Historic Waterways Scenes
BRITAIN'S LOST WATERWAYS
1: Inland Navigations

Two narrow boats at the Little
Tunnel on the top part of the
Basingstoke Canal, probably taken in
1904 or 1905. (See also Plate 56.)

HISTORIC WATERWAYS SCENES

BRITAIN'S LOST WATERWAYS

Volume I, Inland Navigations

Michael E Ware

MOORLAND PUBLISHING

British Library Cataloguing in Publication Data

Ware, Michael Edward
    Britain's lost waterways.
    Vol. I: Inland navigations. – (Historic Waterways
    Scenes; 1).
    1. Canals – Great Britain – History – Pictorial Works
    I. Title
    386'.46'0941   HE435
    ISBN 0–903485–68–0

ISBN 0 903485 68 0

Photoset by Advertiser Printers Ltd, Newton Abbot
and printed in Great Britain
by Redwood Burn Ltd, Trowbridge & Esher
for Moorland Publishing Co Ltd,
PO Box 2, Ashbourne, Derbyshire, DE6 1DZ

Learning Centre Survey

Have your say by visiting Learning Centre Online & clicking the **SURVEY** button!

You can choose to enter our £250 prize draw, top prize is £100 to spend in major high street stores

LEEDS METROPOLITAN UNIVERSITY

CONTENTS

ACKNOWLEDGEMENTS

So many people have helped with this volume that it would not be possible to list them all. First and foremost thanks must go to Edward Paget-Tomlinson for so kindly reading everything that was written, correcting it in many places and as usual adding many interesting and absorbing facts. Many people with local knowledge checked the pages on their particular waterways. In particular I would like to thank Major C.B. Grundy, Brian Waters, Peter Norton, Alan Faulkner, David Robinson, John Goodchild, David McDougal, and the staff of the Ironbridge Gorge Museum Trust. Michael Sedgwick corrected the grammatical mistakes while Paulette Hitchin not only wrote over 550 research letters but typed the manuscript at least twice. I am very grateful to my wife Janet, for all the helpful comments she has made, and the encouragement she has given me. Much inspiration and help has been gained from Ronald Russell's excellent book *Lost Canals of England and Wales*.

As to the picture research, this has been done over a two-year period during which time I must have looked at well over 60,000 photographs. There are 30,000 pictures in the Francis Frith Collection alone, and I went right through them thanks to the enthusiasm of John Buck. As for those million photographs in the National Monument Record, I can only claim to have scraped the surface. Richard Hutchings, until recently Curator of the Waterways Museum at Stoke Bruerne, gave much encouragement and lent many photographs from that museum's collection.

As you will see from the list below the photographs have come from a very wide range of sources: private individuals, canal societies, museums, libraries, record offices, commercial picture agencies, etc. To all those who have helped, thank you very much. To those of you who have helped, but whose pictures were not used, I can only say sorry, and thank you all the same.

The author and publisher are grateful to the following for the use of illustrations:
J. Anderson: 80; Mrs J. Beech: 69, 70; Birmingham Museum of Science and Industry: 31; Black Country Museum: 44; Bradford Central Library: 127, 128; British Rail, Midland Region: 114; British Rail, Western Region: 26, 60, 61, 62, 63; J.E. Brownlow: 85; Derby Museum: 15; Derby Public Library: 12, 13; Derbyshire Record Office: 16, 97; John Dickinson & Co Ltd: 141; Dudley Canal Trust: 42; Dudley Public Library: 46, (T.W. King Collection): 40, 45, 47; Francis Frith Collection: 1, 33, 111; W.K.V. Gale: 41; Grantham Library: 81; A.R. Griffin: 2; Alan Griffiths: 140; Charles Hadfield: 88; Hampshire County Museums Service: 48, 49, 50; Harmsworth Family Collection: 52, 58; H. Harris: 79; Hereford Library: 64, 65; A. Hulme: 136; Ironbridge Gorge Museum Trust: 76, 78; E. Jones (via Lady Markham): 116, 117, 118; Kendal Library: 108, 112; G. Knapp, 82; Leicester Museums: 132; Peter Lewis: 67, 68; Mack of Manchester Ltd: 137; C. Makepeace: 105; Eric de Maré: 29; Hugh McKnight Collection: 34, 35, 36, 37, 71, 83, 87, 102, 103, 107, 109, 110, 113, 139; National Coal Board: 3; National Monument Record: 73, 125; Peter Norton: 95; H. Northern: *Frontis*, , 53, 56; *Old Motor:* 77; H.W. Plant:135; C.L.M. Porter: 91, 92, 93, 94; Rochdale Canal Company: 21, 22; Rochdale Metropolitan Borough Library: 17, 23, 24, 25; Frank Rodgers: 11, 14, 84, 99, 100; L.T.C. Rolt archives: 27, 28, 38; Stafford Museum: 126; Surrey and Hampshire Canal Society Archives: 51; Mrs Temple Thurston: 30; City of Wakefield Metropolitan District Archives, Goodchild loan MSS: 4, 6, 7, 9; Waterways Museum, Stoke Bruerne: 32, 66, 74, 75, 98, 101, 103, 106, 115, 119, 121, 123, 124, 129, 130, 131; Reginald Wood: 18, 19, 20. Illustrations not otherwise acknowledged are from the author's collection.

PREFACE

An author of books of this sort is lucky; he can make his own rules. That is all very well; but he must also explain the rules to the readers, if he and his publisher are not to be inundated with letters from canal enthusiasts saying that their favourite piece of waterway has been omitted. These books were to have been entitled 'Forgotten Waterways', but it was soon realised that this would upset all those hard workers who are currently striving to re-open long disused canals and other navigations. Rude reviews would be written (they still may be, of course!) in club or association journals.

The rough criterion for a waterway's inclusion in the book is that it has been closed at one time or another. In some cases the closure may not have been official. In a number of cases, I am pleased to say, the canals have subsequently been re-opened to traffic. Wherever possible the canals have been depicted in the days when they were carrying commercial craft, the traffic for which they were built. In a few cases pictures are included of derelict canals, but in the main these were photographed so long ago as to be of interest to the enthusiast as well as the industrial archaeologist. Only a very few modern pictures of such waterways appear.

In undertaking my research I tried to find sources of illustrations for practically every canal which has closed. Having gathered them all together I found it quite impossible to illustrate each one and anyway this process would have been repetitive in the extreme. I have therefore chosen those pictures which in my opinion best reflect the overall scene, even if this meant the inclusion of a disproportionate number from any one individual canal. I hope I have included your favourite but if I have not, then blame it on these rules.

I think I must have written to most of the societies and associations which are connected with closed waterways. I have received many helpful and knowledgeable replies. I have been surprised, though, at the number of societies who do not appear to have a member whose job it is to research and collect historic items of print or illustration. My request to one society nearly produced solicitor's letters between two members who did hold such photographs but for internal political reasons found themselves unable to make them available! If these books do nothing else, I hope they will make such societies more aware of this particular branch of waterway history. The collection of such material is best done in collaboration with the local history society, library, museum, or county records office; thus the maximum benefit will result to all.

Because of the amount of material collected this work will appear in two parts. Those canals and navigations which are basically internal are included in this volume. The second part will contain those navigations which go down to the sea, and will include the canals of South Wales and the waterways which link the River Thames with the Severn and its estuary.

In this book I have drawn on two major works of reference, quoting extensively from each. Of these Priestley's *Navigable Rivers and Canals*, first published in 1831, gives an account of each canal and railway for the construction of which an Act of Parliament was passed in or before 1830. Secondly, *Bradshaw's Canals and Navigable Rivers of England and Wales* by Henry Rodolph de Salis; this was first published in 1904, and lists all canals which were navigable in that year, giving details of the route, locks, wharves, tunnels, junctions and most other topographical features, as well as the principal dimensions of the boats that could trade on them. To do this de Salis, who was a director of the canal carrying company Fellows Morton and Clayton, travelled over 14,000 miles by water, mainly in his steam launch *Dragon Fly*. These trips took him 11 years. Little credit has been given to de Salis as a photographer, and while he may not have been technically very efficient, many of the pictures he took on this trip have survived. They are in the collection of Hugh McKnight and a number are used in this book. Very few working boatmen kept a diary, hence for descriptions of trips on canals in the last century or early in this we must rely on the accounts of a few upper class travellers who took to the canals for a holiday. I have quoted from E. Temple Thurston's book *The Flower of Gloster*, an account of such a trip in 1908. His widow is happily still alive and has allowed me access to the photographic record of his trip. (All three of these books have been made available in recent years as reprints by David and Charles of Newton Abbot).

INTRODUCTION

When the Duke of Bridgewater's Canal was opened in 1761 the price of coal in Manchester is reputed to have fallen from 7d to 4d a hundredweight. We can marvel at the actual prices quoted but this drop of nearly 50 per cent in the charges demonstrates better than anything else the effect the canal had on the urban population of Manchester. It is a pity the coming of North Sea oil has not had a similar effect on our life today.

Before the advent of the canal system overland transport in Britain had been very difficult. The Romans had given us a first-rate road system, but once they had left there was no central government to take responsibility for it. A need for trade has always existed although for many years it was confined to essentials such as salt, wool or corn. The roads were so poor that coal would normally only be carried for a few miles around the colliery or bellpit. Packhorse trains could not carry any great quantity of materials although they could traverse poor roads. Any form of cart required a reasonable surface on which to travel.

River navigation was important but because of floods and rapids most rivers needed artificial attention to allow boats to travel any real distance inland. If we take the Thames as an example, by the early Middle Ages it was navigable only as far as Richmond, and even by 1660 Oxford marked the upper limit. The Thames above Oxford was to be a tricky navigation until the 1900s. One of the biggest problems with rivers was the presence of mills, each of which required a head of water to operate. Understandably, millers were reluctant to let the water impounded behind their dam or weir flow freely just to allow a barge to pass up or down stream.

The Duke of Bridgewater's canal from his coalmines at Worsley was not the country's first artificial waterway but it was the start of the great Midland system — Trent and Mersey, Staffordshire and Worcestershire, etc. There is no denying the Bridgewater's effect on industry and local people around Manchester. Coal could travel over the 11-mile canal day and night with virtually no hindrance from weather, mill owners or other disruptions. Even while this canal was being built industrialists were recognising its potential, and its engineers, John Gilbert and James Brindley, were in great demand for new projects. Within the next forty years or so 'canal mania' set in. Nearly every city, town or village wanted a waterway. It is interesting to note that Parliament looked enthusiastically on the majority of the projects, as the Canal Acts came before them. They fully realised that if private enterprise did not do it, they might be asked to subsidise some of them from Government funds. Many were built, but equally many were never started; other projects were started but never completed. The Southampton to Salisbury canal and the Leominster canal would be good examples of the latter. The canals held sway until the early 1850s, by which time the railways had become firmly established. Many of the canal companies had only themselves to blame for the loss of much of their trade to the railways. For fifty or so years they had enjoyed a monopoly. Some had charged high tolls, or had paid excellent dividends to the shareholders. Many had ploughed insufficient money back into maintenance or had failed to plan for expansion; in other words, complacency set in. Telford is reputed to have made the following comment in the 1820s on the state of the Birmingham canals, saying that they had become

. . . little better than a crooked ditch, with scarcely the appearance of a towing-path, the horses frequently sliding and staggering in the water, the hauling-lines sweeping the gravel into the canal, and the entanglement at the meeting of boats being incessant; whilst at the locks at each end of the short summit at Smethwick crowds of boatmen were always quarrelling, or offering premiums for a preference of passage; and the mine-owners, injured by the delay, were loud in their just complaints . . .

In the 1820s or 1830s, under Telford's direction, the Birmingham main line was greatly improved, deepened and widened; for once money was being ploughed back. The great works which took place on the Grand Union between London and Birmingham in the 1930s came a hundred years too late. Through no fault of their own, the different gauges of numerous neighbouring waterways were a cause of extra expense to traders, and had Brindley and his associates shown greater foresight, the locks on his first cross country waterway, the Trent and Mersey, would not have been fixed at 7 feet by 72 feet, so laying down the dimensions of the traditional narrow boat, which in later years had great difficulty in surviving as an economic proposition.

The view has been expressed that the Duke of Bridgewater exercised some influence over the size of locks on the Trent and Mersey and some other canals. The Duke wanted to secure the cargoes by transhipment from the smaller narrow boats into his bigger Mersey flats at Preston Brook, for onward transmission to Liverpool. It must be remembered that there was also a substantial mileage of canal and river navigation designed for larger craft, such as keels, flats, trows, etc.

Another problem was that the canal companies were not allowed to run fleets of cargo boats on their own canals. They had to rely on tolls from private traders. In 1847 this law was changed, but not all the companies took advantage of it. Those that did found in the main that they could improve their incomes by becoming carriers.

At first, narrow boats had an all-male crew who lived on the bank overnight. Later the boatmen had to take his family from the bank and put them on the boat. Here all of them were set to work, thus dispensing with the services of a mate. The family did, however, have to work unnaturally long hours — sometimes seven days a week as well — to make ends meet. From this progression we can see that the private trader was gradually forced off the water.

At first the railways were only interested in passenger traffic and the carriage of light goods, neither of which was a real threat to the waterways, who ran relatively few packet or passenger boats. Soon, however, the rail directors realised that heavy goods and mineral traffic would bring in a good revenue; then came the real clash between the two transport systems. I think it is true to say that for quite a number of years waterways kept those old customers who were on the canalside, but new factories, collieries, etc, tended to be rail-connected if this was at all possible. It was the country canals which suffered first.

They had never carried high tonnages; therefore tolls were low and so was income in relation to expenditure. The coming of the country railway hit them hard; one should remember that it has only been in the recent past that the daily pick-up goods train has departed our railways, and a daily rail connection for agricultural products is far better than slow delivery by canal.

Canals could compete as long as cargoes could be loaded directly into the boats and off-loaded direct into the factory at the other end; as long, also, as speed was of secondary importance. If a factory's requirement was 25 tons of coal a day, it did not really matter how long it took that coal to reach the factory provided the supply was regular and prices competitive. Unlike the railways, canals were often affected by weather conditions in the winter, and ice-breaking was a major part of a maintenance gang's work at such times. The waterway could be held up for weeks while the railways were relatively unaffected. Structural repairs did not usually disrupt a railway for more than a day or two, but lock or bridge repairs could

close a canal for weeks on end. It must also be realised that although there were 4,000 miles of canal in 1860, there were a good 7,500 miles of railway at that time.

Although the Turnpike Acts of the 1800s led to substantial improvements, roads were not used for regular long distance heavy haulage until the 1920s, by which time the motor lorry was firmly established. The lorry was the death-blow to the canal system as far as commercial traffic was concerned in the Midlands and the South. A certain amount of coal, oil, and other products are, however, still a regular traffic on river navigations in the north-east.

These, then, were some of the pressures on the canals, and the reasons why so many closed. These two books try to capture the feel of the commercial waterway system by looking at canals which have closed or have been abandoned, and which in many cases have been all but obliterated by subsequent development.

1

1 Most of the Bridgewater Canal as originally built is still very much with us and in use, but one small section, now derelict, was very important. As we have seen, the purpose of the waterway was to bring coal from Worsley into Manchester. At first the coal was mined in the conventional way from above. Drainage is always a problem in mines and here a drainage sough (tunnel) was built from the base of the workings out of the nearby hillside at Worsley into the Worsley Brook. With the coming of the canal to Worsley this sough was made navigable so that boats could be taken right into the mines. To work within the restricted confines of these mines a new type of boat was built, known by the slang term 'starvationer'. Their proper title is 'M boats'. The nickname 'starvationer' probably came about because of the very exposed knees within the boat which when unloaded does have the appearance of a skeleton. There were three sizes of boat, the largest being 55 feet long and 4 feet 6 inches wide. It could carry 12 tons on a draught of 2 feet 6 inches. These were the forerunners of the English narrow boat. Coal was mined and placed into containers, and these containers were loaded into the boats. Is nothing new? This scene was taken around the turn of the century at Worsley Delph and shows a number of derelict M boats of different sizes. Mining had ceased in 1887.

2 The historian Samuel Smiles writes of these mines

...the barges are deeply laden with their black freight, which they have brought from the mines through the two low semi-circular arches opening at the base of the rock, such being the entrances to the underground canals which now extend to nearly 40 miles in all directions.... Where the tunnel passed through earth or coal the arching was of brickwork but where it passed through rock it was simply hewn out.

Trains of between six and twenty boats at a time would be taken into the mine. There were 46 miles of underground canal in all, on four levels including an inclined plane 151 feet long with a slope of one in four. What a frightening place it must have been to work in.

3 The derelict mines these days are looked after by the National Coal Board. This picture, taken in recent years, shows such an NCB inspection party emerging, having undertaken the journey in one of the old M boats. At one time a few visits were arranged in order that industrial archaeologists could inspect these workings, but the mines are said to be so dangerous now that this practice has ceased. At the end of the original length of the Bridgewater Canal in Manchester another tunnel was built. Wharves and warehouses were situated at the basin at Castlefield which was well below the main streets of the city. To save having to tranship the coal to carts and haul it laboriously up the hillside, a ¾ mile tunnel was dug into the side of the hill, and at a point near Deansgate a vertical shaft was sunk to connect with the tunnel below. The boats from Worsley were taken into the underground tunnels and 8 cwt containers unloaded by means of a crane pulling them up the shaft. Power for the crane was supplied by a waterwheel. The rate of unloading is said to have been 5 tons of cargo every half hour, which was handled by two men and a boy.

4 The Barnsley Canal left the Aire and Calder main line via Heath Lock, a mile downstream from Wakefield. With the Dearne and Dove Canal it provided a route through the prosperous South Yorkshire coalfields from the Aire and Calder to the Don Navigation. It was completed through to Barnsley in 1799; an extension right into the coal-producing area beyond to Barnby basin was opened three years later. Priestley, writing in his *Navigable Rivers and Canals* published in 1831, says,

this canal was projected principally with the view of opening the very valuable and extensive coal fields in the neighbourhood of Barnsley and Silkstone, and its execution has had the effect of introducing the coal, worked in the latter place, into the London Market, where it holds a distinguished place amongst the Yorkshire coals.

Here we see an empty Yorkshire keel rising out of Heath Lock at the entrance to the canal around the turn of this century. The lock-cum-toll keeper lived in the house; the building on the left houses the canalside stables; we see a horse coming out of one of them. The boat horse is being led by a 'horse marine' as the horsemen were always known in Yorkshire. Keels often had a coggie boat or rowing boat with them for use on tidal waters. As these were not used when trading on canals, some visiting keels have left theirs tied to the bank on the right of the picture.

CONNECTING CANALS

Most canals were planned individually. Completely separate companies were set up and there was great rivalry between them. It was not until they were in existence that some of the rivalry eased, and the advantages could be seen in making sure that trade could flow from one waterway to another and from one part of the country to another. In some cases the companies were pig-headed and situations such as that at Worcester Bar came into being. Here the Worcester and Birmingham Canal was not allowed to join the Birmingham Canal Navigations; a stretch of wharf a few yards wide was left between them, and all on-going cargoes had to be transhipped. Canal companies were always jealous of their water and when a new canal wharf joined an established one it was usually made to come in at a higher level via the entrance lock. In this way the established canal always obtained a lock full of water as each boat passed through the lock. The stop locks at Hawkesbury Junction (Oxford Canal with the Coventry Canal) and Autherley Junction (Shropshire Union Canal with the Staffordshire and Worcestershire Canal) are possibly the best examples. At Hawkesbury both canals had their own stop lock and both locks had a drop of only a few inches.

Even though they were not all connecting canals the waterways of Birmingham have been included in this section. These are really so interesting and intricate that they require a full length pictorial book of their own. It has often been quoted that there were many more miles of canal in Birmingham and the Black Country than there were in Venice. Be that as it may, the Midlands Canals were very important indeed and in general terms carried more traffic than almost any other waterway in this country.

5

5   Here is a view down the Aire and Calder main line, with Heath Lock toll house and the Barnsley Canal on the right. A non-tidal Yorkshire keel, most probably loaded with coal, has just left the lock. At this point the tow path of the Aire and Calder navigation was on the far bank (out of the picture on the left-hand side). The boat tied up in the foreground (extreme left) is the ferry used by boatmen to bring their horses across should they be going from the Aire and Calder onto the Barnsley Canal. The date is around 1905. The Silkstone Collieries provided much of the traffic on the canal in earlier days; this coal had to be taken by cart on the local roads to the canal head. Due to the appalling state of these roads there were often hold-ups and it was not unusual to find up to ten boats waiting at the basin for their cargoes to arrive. Later this fault was overcome by the building of a horse-drawn plateway to the canal. Some say the delay was also caused by poor output at the coal face — whatever the reason, boat owners could not afford serious delays such as this.

6   This photograph, taken around 1900, is of the Heath flight of locks with two Yorkshire keels passing. The nearer of the two vessels is one of the Aire and Calder's own carrying fleet, which were numbered but not named, and is returning empty or at least lightly loaded. Keel captains would always try to obtain the back carriage of a cargo if they possibly could. In the earlier years of the canal, limestone formed an important back loading against the down flow of coal. Possibly the white substance in the hold of the loaded boat seen here is limestone. Lime kilns were established on the sides of the canals, and some coalmasters took the opportunity to burn off their slack in these kilns. Tidal keels always towed from the neddy (towing mast) stepped in the lutchet; non-tidal versions swapped their masts from side to side depending on the towing path. It can be seen that Number 42 has laid the neddy flat and is towing from the lutchet, while the keel coming up has the neddy erect, presumably to counteract her lowness in the water. The canal had been taken over by the Aire and Calder Navigation in 1854 and later they worked traffic of up to 272,000 tons in one year.

7   Water was a problem on the Barnsley Canal. Originally an 80 acre reservoir was built at Cold Hindley, which in later years was augmented by the building of another one nearby at Wintersett. Unusually, this Cornish pumping engine at Ryhill pumping station was used to take water out of the canal whenever there was a surplus and pump it back into the reservoir for future use. The beam engine came from Harveys of Hayle and was most probably bought second-hand from a disused Cornish copper mine. It was by no means worn out, as it continued in use until the closure of the canal in 1946. Mining subsidence was a problem in the area; in 1911 the Barnsley aqueduct was affected and had to be closed for repairs for eight months. Again in 1945 there was trouble near the aqueduct. Mottram Wood colliery was flooded, and compensation had to be paid. In November 1946 the canal burst its banks at Littleworth and that really was the end, although abandonment did not come until 1953. This photograph is thought to have been taken around 1910.

11 Reservoir Engine House
Ryhill.

8 This fine engraving of a colliery scene is of Edmund Main colliery to the south of Barnsley on the Worsborough branch of the Dearne and Dove Canal, opened in 1804. The sketch is dated 1859. If this drawing was taken from life, why, one wonders, did the artist depict the trading boats as having sails? Could it have been that he saw keels with masts which he thought were for sails? The boats are clearly meant to be keels, but they would only sail on canals if the wind conditions really suited them, and then only with a small square sail on a short mast. In canal work it was normal for keels to leave masts and lee boards on the bank, say at Doncaster. While coal was one of the chief traffics on the Dearne and Dove, it was also its downfall. This branch had to be closed in 1906 because of mining subsidence and parts of the canal were only 4 feet 6 inches deep when they should have been 6 feet deep, due to this same problem. The Elsecar branch was closed for the same reason in 1928.

9 The branch of the Dearne and Dove to the Elsecar basin was only just over two miles long, but had a rise of six locks. It was built principally to serve collieries. Unfortunately the date of this photograph is not known but it is a most interesting scene in the basin at Elsecar. The keel on the left has arrived loaded with pit props, while the one behind appears to be empty. These keels were fitted with close-fitting hatch boards (covers) to keep the cargoes dry from both rain and tidal water, but they often covered non-perishable cargoes as well. The covers have a very distinct curve on them which allows unladen boats the maximum amount of room under low bridges such as those on the section of the Sheffield Canal, an extension of the Don Navigation. The keel in the foreground has had its rudder lengthened to help with manoeuverability on the canals. It is also fitted with a special canal tiller bent up and over the rail. Such a tiller helps when rounding sharp bends as an ordinary one would foul the stanchions. The hefty rope in the

coggie or cock boat in the foreground shows that the keels were used for trading on tidal waterways. The clinker planking of the two keels in the foreground tells us that they were built no later than the mid-19th century.

10 For once it is possible to illustrate a way in which canal water can be used to help a coalmine; usually the mines are blamed for subsidence which causes havoc with the banks and beds of waterways. There was a serious explosion at Edmund Main colliery in December 1862 when fifty-nine men and boys were killed. The owners were unable to extinguish the ensuing fire, and eventually a channel was dug from the nearby canal and the water used to flood the pit.

8

11 The line of the Derby Canal is shaped like an inverted 'V' with Derby at the apex. One arm of the canal connects with the Erewash Canal at Sandiacre, and the other end with the Trent and Mersey at Swarkestone junction — about the only point, incidentally, where the canal can be clearly seen these days. Opened in 1796, it enjoyed some through trade, but most of it went to Derby. Otherwise it was traffic from the Little Eaton branch canal — mainly coal. An interesting aspect of the canal was its crossing of the River Derwent in Derby itself. The canal crossed the river on the level just upstream of an unusual semi-circular weir. In order that the tow path could also cross, a narrow timber bridge was built. In times of flood it shielded the narrow boats from being swept over the weir but it was often being damaged itself due to the build-up of water-borne flood debris. Pedestrians were allowed to use the bridge as long as they did not 'wheel perambulators or barrows that may impede the passage of horses'. It became unsafe in 1950 and was finally demolished in 1959.

12 The coming of the canal led to the opening up of a number of waterside arms and wharves off the River Derwent itself. Just above the canal crossing there was another weir across the river, but this was by-passed by a short lock cut for water-borne traffic wanting to reach the wharves of the leadshot producing company of Cox Brothers, part of Morledge Leadworks situated on the Markeaton brook leading down to the river. Here the brook has been made navigable for Trent-type barges; one of these and a narrow boat are seen loading. The shot tower, incidentally, was built in 1809 and was demolished in 1931. Tenant Bridge is in the foreground.

13 The first lock up from the river crossing on the south side was Pegg's Flood Lock, an unusually shaped lock as the gates were at either end of a wharf area. Under normal circumstances the gates of this lock were kept open. If the river was in flood then the bottom gate would be shut to hold the river water back — the gates were mitred the opposite way to normal for this purpose. This photograph, taken in August 1874, shows Days Lock, the next one up the canal, a few hundred yards above Peggs Flood Lock. Though the fall through this lock is not very great, it too can be operated as a flood lock. In this picture it is in use in the normal way. Should flood water come up the canal from Peggs (out of the picture down the canal to the left), the extra pair of gates shown in the foreground could be closed to protect the canal above. The house on the right is the toll-and-lock keeper's cottage. One upstairs window is set noticeably higher up under the roof. This would have been the window from which the toll keeper watched for approaching traffic.

11

14 For many years the Derby Canal Company tried to sell itself to a railway company; there were, however, no takers. But before it suffered at the hands of railway competition, it had handled as much as 200,000 tons of cargo in a year, a good performance by most standards. The company tried to close the canal in the 1920s, but never actually got round to doing it. After World War II the canal was allowed to abandon itself even though officially it did not close until 1964. The canal company remained in being until June 1974, and this is a photograph of their Bridgewater Wharf in Derby. The warehouse on the right with the crane was built in 1820, and along with all the other buildings in the wharf area was demolished in July 1975. This picture was taken about 1960; the derelict craft was an ice-breaker. The photograph was taken from Cattle Market Bridge, under which once stood what was probably the first cast-iron aqueduct. It was designed by Benjamin Outram to carry the canal over an earlier cut by George Sorocold.

15

15 The Canal Tavern was situated in Cockpit Hill, approximately 200 yards from the canal wharf in Derby itself. Nearby were two other pubs, The Castle and Falcon, and The Boat. All three were demolished in the late 1960s during clearance to make way for the new Eagle Shopping Centre. This picture is thought to date from the early 1930s. The bus is a 1927 Gilford, and behind it is a splendidly ornate urinal. The public house was an important part of the boatman's life, particularly in horsedrawn days. Most canalside pubs had stables. This one, for example, offers 'good stabling' where the horse could be left overnight. The pub was the only form of recreation that boatmen would normally get; most would be working long hours and possibly six or even seven days a week as well. It would be wrong, however, to assume that the boatman's life was one long pub crawl. There would be many occasions when he could not afford even a beer in the tavern. As the canals lost their commercial traffic and closed down, so did many of the pubs, as they had no alternative market to draw on. A few situated near roads and bridges could turn their backs on the canal and try and tempt car and coach traffic. Some of these have recently turned round again, and now obtain their trade from passing pleasure boats!

16 The part which the tramway played in the first hundred odd years of the canal system has received insufficient attention from writers. At one time there were over 1,500 miles of horsedrawn waggon or tramway in England and Wales, a large proportion of which led from quarries, mines or works down to navigable water of some sort, usually a canal or river. In many cases canals were originally designed to connect with such a tramway, usually because the terrain was difficult and it was cheaper to build a tramway than extend the canal. The Little Eaton Gangway from the Derby Canal was typical. In the original Canal Act it said '. . . and for making Railways from such canal to several collieries. . . .' Further on the Act says 'And also to make and maintain a Rail or Wagon Way or Stone Road for the conveyance of coal, iron, ironstone, lead ore, limestone and other articles . . .

from the termination of the canal at Little Eaton aforesaid. . . .' The gangway's principal cargo was coal from Denby and Kilburn collieries. The coal was loaded into containers, each box containing 33-8 cwt. At Little Eaton Wharf the gangs of loaded trams were positioned in such a way that the wharf crane could unload them into the waiting narrow boats. The Little Eaton Company was one of the last to close, and this picture of pointwork by the Wharf was taken in 1908, a year before closure.

17 The state of the roads over the Pennines from Manchester to Yorkshire in the mid 1700s can be imagined, so it is not surprising that one of the first canal schemes mooted in the north would follow that route. It took a long time, however, before the Rochdale Canal became a *fait accompli,* and it was not until 1804 that it was opened from Manchester through to join the Calder and Hebble at Sowerby Bridge. The canal was built to wide dimensions of 14 feet 2 inches and the locks were 72 feet in length, so most types of northern inland trading craft could traverse it. Here we see a pair of narrow boats breasted up at Clegg Hall, Littleborough. These narrow boats were deep (six planks instead of the usual five) and could be said to be clumsy. The gang plank at the forend rests on a stand and not a triangular cratch as is more common on the Midland narrow boat. The date of the picture is not known, neither is it known why the boats are facing in opposite directions!

18 One of the most successful traders on the Rochdale Canal was William Jackson, who in 1845 had over 30 barges or flats trading. It is interesting to see that he also had 120 horses, which averages out at 4 per boat, the reason for this high number being that fly boats (express boats) required frequent changes of horses, and many spare horses were always kept. In 1891 he sold out to the Rochdale Canal Company. In 1894 two of these boats were bought by Albert Wood of Sowerby Bridge. This photograph, taken at Castleton near Rochdale in 1907, shows Albert Wood's Mersey flat *Bedford,* typical of the craft which would have traded in the area. Such boats were a very tight fit into the locks, hence the elaborate sets of fenders — both sill and stem types. This would have been a family boat with accommodation fore and aft.

19 Some of Albert Wood's boatmen and boat horses photographed in May 1912 at the Peak Forest Wharf of Ducie Street Basin, Manchester, headquarters of the Rochdale Canal Company. Albert Wood continued trading until 1919. Both this and the previous photographs come from the collection of Reginald Wood, seen as a child sitting between the two ladies near the stern of *Bedford* in Plate 18.

20

21

20 The Rochdale Canal Company started trading in its own right in the 1880s, continuing through until July 1921. This is the final bale of the last load of cotton brought by *Primrose* to Lock Hill Mill, Sowerby Bridge, a month before the carrying fleet was disbanded. The horse is fully harnessed and ready to leave as soon as this bale is unloaded and the photographer has left. The date was 3 June 1921. These craft were designed to take 80-90 tons of cargo on a 5 feet draft, but few canals could provide this. The Rochdale Canal was hardly ever over 4 feet in depth during the early part of this century, so the maximum cargo carried would only be around 40 tons. The tonnage on this canal reached the staggering total of just under a million tons in the year 1845, just before the coming of real railway competition. A lot of this, however, was short haul traffic off the Bridgewater Canal.

21 The Rochdale Company gave their boats the names of flowers or girls. They were gaily painted in a red, white and pale blue livery. The hawse ports were called eyes, and continuing the analogy of a face, the rubbing strakes below were called whiskers. In this case the boat has been unloaded, the hatchboards have been refitted, covering the cargo hold, and the hatch cloths would normally be secured by battens, wedges and lashings. The stacked hatch boards are clearly seen on the boat behind and there are others on the wharf to the left.

22 *Emily* was one of the Calder and Hebble style keels or 'west country' boats operated by the Rochdale Canal Company and is seen here near Mirfield. Such boats were usually crewed by two people, who worked the boat itself. The third member was a horse marine, who was hired along with the horse. In this case the captain was one James Shaw, while the mate was Arthur Shaw. The horse marine was A. Wainhouse. The name of the horse is not recorded but it had the number 175. The last complete run over the full length of the canal was in 1937, and navigation was abandoned in 1952. Somehow the Rochdale Canal remained independent and was not nationalised in 1948, and while it received no income from tolls from passing boats, it was able to continue as a property company. Dale Street basin was filled in and used as a car park which provided a useful revenue also, although this area is now scheduled for redevelopment. The canal is open again from Castlefield Junction with the Bridgewater Canal through the heart of Manchester to Ducie Street Junction with the Ashton Canal and is part of the popular cruising route 'The Cheshire Ring'. The Ducie Street to Sowerby Bridge section of the canal is being worked on by a group of enthusiasts, with the help of the Government Job Creation Scheme, and eventually it is hoped to re-open it right through, although this will be an expensive business, due to alterations which have taken place to the canal bed with road widening, etc.

23

TESTIN FIR GROVE BRIDGE
MILNROW

24

TESTING FIR GROVE BRIDGE
MILNROW

23 and 24 An unusual aspect of canal maintenance — bridge testing after rebuilding on the Rochdale Canal. As many motorists know to their cost, a lot of canal bridges are hump backed, the reason for this being that the engineers, when building the canal, saved money by skimping with the length of the embankments leading up to the bridge on either side. Some canal Acts specified a length for these in order to eliminate or lessen the hump. In 1906 Firgrove Bridge, narrow, cobbled and humped, had been replaced by a wider and more easily graded structure. Before opening it for traffic the engineers are submitting it to tests, using two traction engines as a moveable load.

25 The annual outing of the local church, Sunday School or other similar group was often photographed and presumably prints sold or given to the participants. To many children this annual 'treat' would be the highlight of the year. Sometimes it took the form of a journey in horse drawn vehicles; other photographs show the people in carts behind traction engines. Where a canal passed through the neighbourhood, it was not unusual for a trading boat to be taken over for a day. Benches and people would be substituted for cargo. This is a Calder and Hebble size keel, or West Country boat, with the Littleborough Parish Church school outing around 1910, on the Rochdale Canal. The photographer has caught a miscreant throwing stones into the canal to splash the occupants.

26 Canal companies have always been very jealous of their water supplies. When canals of different companies joined, they usually insisted upon a stop lock being built, although in the majority of cases there was only a slight difference in the levels. Such a lock would prevent one company, in the event of a burst, drawing water from the other, or just letting its water level fall, and recouping from the opposition. Often the lock was in favour of the older canal which then gained a shallow lock full of water with each boat. Usually the stop lock was supervised by two men, one employed by each company; the gates were kept shut and only opened for the passage of craft. At Kings Norton junction, a pair of guillotine gates were installed near the junction of the Stratford-upon-Avon Canal and the Worcester & Birmingham Canal. Guillotine gates were used as they held back the water either side of the lock and it did not matter which of the canals had the higher level at any one time. Here, in the 1920s, the Kings Norton Lock is in full working order and the counter balance weight is clearly shown. Though these gates still survive, they are retained purely as an industrial relic.

-EBORO'PARISH CHURCH SCHOOL ANNUAL TRIP. "ON THE VOYAGE"

27 and **28** The Stratford-upon-Avon Canal is now divided into two parts. The northern section to Lapworth (Kingswood Junction) has never officially closed, but the Great Western Railway stopped navigation on it for some five years by repairing Lifford Bridge in such a way that it could not be opened by boatmen. Canal enthusiasts owe a great debt of gratitude to the work done by the Inland Waterways Association, founded in 1946 by Robert Aickman. In 1947 Lord Methuen asked a question in the House of Lords about the fixing of Lifford Bridge and was told that the bridge 'would be lifted at any time on notice of intending passage being given.' Tom Rolt, first General Secretary of the Inland Waterways Association, gave notice of intent to navigate the canal in his narrow boat *Cressy*, adding that he wished to pass under the bridge on 20 May 1947. The Great Western Railway provided a narrow boat to go ahead to clear the way in case of trouble with the derelict waterway. This boat, however, got stuck and *Cressy* was on her own. With much bow-hauling and effort *Cressy* got through to the bridge, which the railway gangers had lifted with jacks and rested on baulks of timber.

28

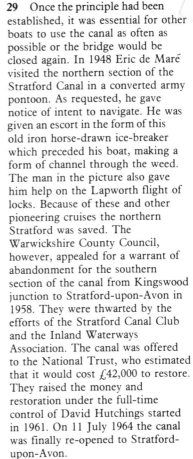

29 Once the principle had been established, it was essential for other boats to use the canal as often as possible or the bridge would be closed again. In 1948 Eric de Maré visited the northern section of the Stratford Canal in a converted army pontoon. As requested, he gave notice of intent to navigate. He was given an escort in the form of this old iron horse-drawn ice-breaker which preceded his boat, making a form of channel through the weed. The man in the picture also gave him help on the Lapworth flight of locks. Because of these and other pioneering cruises the northern Stratford was saved. The Warwickshire County Council, however, appealed for a warrant of abandonment for the southern section of the canal from Kingswood junction to Stratford-upon-Avon in 1958. They were thwarted by the efforts of the Stratford Canal Club and the Inland Waterways Association. The canal was offered to the National Trust, who estimated that it would cost £42,000 to restore. They raised the money and restoration under the full-time control of David Hutchings started in 1961. On 11 July 1964 the canal was finally re-opened to Stratford-upon-Avon.

30 Trade on the section from Kingswood Junction to Stratford-upon-Avon, opened in 1816, gradually declined in the twentieth century, and the section was unfit for traffic by 1940. Temple Thurston took this charming picture of one of the picturesque barrel-roofed lock houses when he travelled the canal. In his well-known book *Flower of Gloster*, first published in 1911, he comments on the traffic

... sometimes, they tell me, a barge makes its solitary way down to Stratford, but the locks have in the crevices of their gates all that luxuriant growth of waterweed which shows you how seldom they are used. ...

This lock cottage is at Lowsonford; the scene has changed very little and is still a popular one with photographers.

31 Some 5½ miles above Stratford is the largest single engineering work on the lower part of the canal, the Edstone or Bearley aqueduct. In the history books this is quite overshadowed by the Pontcysyllte. Nevertheless it is one of the largest cast-iron aqueducts of its type in the country, its total length being 475 feet; it stands 28 feet above the valley at the highest point. The valley contains a road, a stream, and two railway lines. This photograph shows the structure in apparently good repair and full of water in the mid 1920s. Like the pioneer iron aqueduct at Longdon-on-Tern the towing path is constructed alongside the waterway and not over it, as at Pontcysyllte. The car owner's appreciation of good engineering is shown by his choice of vehicle, a 21 hp Lanchester of about 1924.

32 The canal came under the control of the railway in 1856; when it later came under the wing of the GWR they incorporated an unusual means of watering their locomotives. Instead of the traditional watertower or water crane, locomotives using the Alcester branch could stop under the aqueduct and draw water direct from it. The valve controlling the flow is at the bottom of the down pipe. They had a stove mounted under it to stop the pipe freezing up in mid-winter. This photograph was taken after the branch was closed.

34 The Avon between Evesham and Tewkesbury is now known as the Lower Avon. This, too, has recently been restored to full navigation by the Lower Avon Navigation Trust. De Salis in his travels passed along this stretch of river in 1896 in his steam launch *Dragon Fly*. She was 59 feet long, and had a 6 feet 8 inch beam — an ideal size for navigating the majority of the canals of this country. Here *Dragon Fly* is seen tied up to the top gates of Wyre Lock just above Pershore.

33 The Stratford Canal was part of a larger waterway system which included the Warwickshire Avon River. In this way trade from the River Severn at Tewkesbury gained access inland to Stratford-upon-Avon itself. The last boat to use the river between Evesham and Stratford is reputed to have traded in 1873; it belonged to the firm of Spraggs of Evesham. This photograph of Lucy's Lock, the first below Stratford, is thought to have been taken around 1900. As originally constructed, Lucy's Lock had a single chamber with a fall of five feet. The water below the lock was retained by a navigation staunch about ¾ mile further on at a place called Weir Break, now the site of the Upper Avon Navigation Trust's new Weir Break lock. At a later stage the navigation staunch at Weir Break was removed and a second chamber was added at the tail of Lucy's Lock, so that it formed a staircase with a total fall of seven feet four inches. Through the efforts of the Upper Avon Navigation Trust boats can again reach Stratford from Evesham.

35 One of the features of the River Avon was the watergates. This is Cropthorne watergate near Fladbury, photographed by de Salis in 1896. *Dragon Fly* can just be seen nestling against the gate. Here a lock gate is situated in a weir, and for de Salis to proceed upstream the whole of the next reach must be lowered before the gate can be opened. This was often a lengthy process — one lock could take several hours to operate. One would have thought that by the turn of this century such locks would have been done away with, but de Salis writing in Bradshaw in 1904 notes 'there are at present 33 navigation weirs or staunches in existence in England, of which 27 termed staunches are situated in the Fen country or on its tributary rivers — the other 6, which are termed weirs, consist of 4 on the Thames between Oxford and Lechlade, and 2 on the Lower Avon navigation (Warwickshire) between Tewkesbury and Evesham'. In 1961 Cropthorne watergate was destroyed in the course of making the Avon navigable once more.

36 'A navigable canal from Birmingham into the county of Warwick to the canal at Aldersley near Wolverhampton in the county of Stafford with a collateral cut to the coalmines at Wednesbury'. This was the description of the original line of the first part of the Birmingham Canal Navigations. The first stretch to be built from the coalfields of Wednesbury to the BCN Company's own wharf on Suffolk Street was completed on 6 November 1769. The full section of the main line opened on 21 September 1772. The offices of the BCN were situated opposite Paradise Street and behind this impressive frontage were two wharves. These two wharves led off from the area we now call Gas Street Basin. The offices were built in 1773 and demolished in 1913. Later the wharves were drained and filled in. From 1913 to 1939 the BCN had its offices in Daimler House, Suffolk Street, after which time they moved to Sneyd, near Walsall.

37 Here we see coal-laden day boats at the rear of the BCN offices round about 1910. While the BCN had plenty of private traders operating over its waterways the company itself traded vigorously, buying coal from the pits, transporting it, selling it, and even distributing it from the wharves by horse and cart. Difference in freeboard between the loaded and nearly empty boats is clearly shown in this photograph. Note also the anti-theft design of the cabin doors. The slide slid under the guides so that it could not be lifted. There is also a lockable bar across the rear doors.

35

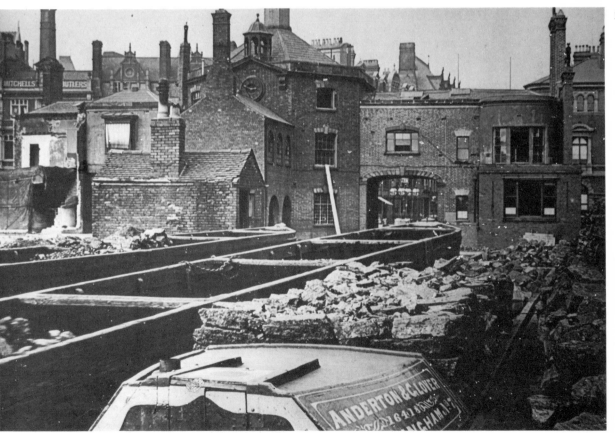

38 The original plan had been for the canal to end at Newhall but this section was built a few years later. The company's headquarters wharf was used for coal traffic and the Newhall wharf for merchandise, àlso for stone and timber. The present day holiday-maker often pauses at the top of Farmer's Bridge flight of locks to spend time in the Long Boat public house. The basin outside the pub is all that is now left of the entrance to the Newhall Canal. In this photograph, taken in 1946 two years before the Newhall section of the canal was closed, we see a group of Fellows, Morton and Clayton boats moored at Cambrian Wharf with the Newhall Canal leading away in the distance. The nearest boat has been built with a small bow cabin where one or two children could have slept. On the left are the Farmer's Bridge locks with a toll keeper's office in the foreground.

39 The Birmingham main line was surveyed and built by James Brindley, who died just a few days after its completion. In true Brindley style it was a contour canal, and at one stage it meandered round Coseley Hill to avoid tunnelling. Later in 1832 the hill was tunnelled through. The only part of this meandering now in use is the section from Deepfields Junction to the British Waterways Board's maintenance yards at Bradley. One of the undertakings served by the section of the canal which has now been filled in was W. Millington and Company's Summer Hill Iron Works. Here we see a number of day boats owned by the Millington Company bringing coal in.

40 This splendid photograph of Bessanna's Basin, Old Hill, was taken in 1918, and shows how coal from Haden's Hill Colliery was brought to the wharf and transhipped. The trams or waggons are not tipper trucks, and have to be physically turned on their side for the coal to be removed. There are no mechanical aids here whatsoever; the coal is all being transhipped by hand. On average it would have taken two men about half a day to load a boat of 25 tons' capacity. In the foreground can be seen a two-handled scoop and a rake. It is generally thought that there was so much traffic from this wharf at this time that some loading had to be undertaken after dark, hence the electric lighting. Many of the Birmingham day boats were pointed at each end and could therefore hang the helm, or 'ellum, at bow or stern. The helm was always taken in board when moored to prevent damage. It was easier to hang in place when resting on the beam.

38

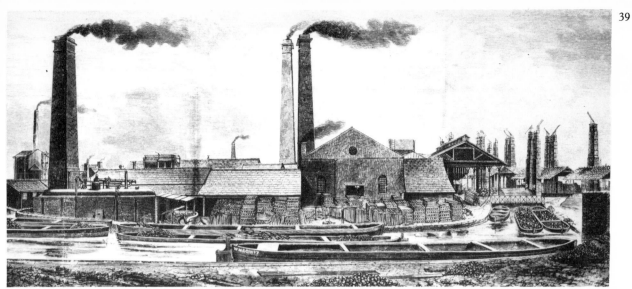

CANAL TUNNEL, DUDLEY CASTLE GROUNDS.

41 This well known picture from the 1920s typifies a busy canal arm to a large industrial works. There were hundreds of such wharves all over the West Midlands. This arm, now filled in, served Alfred Hickman's Spring Vale Furnaces at Bilston. The open day boats brought in coke which was unloaded on the right, the corrugated iron shelters giving some protection to the men working on the wharfside. The irregular shape of the day boats is interesting — they had a very hard life. No great care was ever taken by their steerers, and they were banged into many obstructions — including each other. Surprisingly they seem to have had a life of up to 50 years. On the left, bars of pig iron are stacked awaiting shipment away from the wharf. Possibly the picture was taken on a Sunday as there are very few people in sight. Spring Vale Furnaces were unusual in the Black Country in having a series of nicknames — they were variously known as "The 'ell 'oles", "the 'ot 'oles" or just "'ickmans". The furnaces were no more hot or hellish than any other; the names may have come from Hell Lane nearby. 'Hotholer' was also the name given to some open iron or steel day

boats used for ironworks traffic, so called because of the furnaces. The last of these furnaces was demolished in 1959. The site is now occupied by a modern plant and all traces of the furnaces and the canal basin have disappeared.

42 The Earl of Dudley owned a number of coalmines, some of which were in the area of Pensnett Chase. To serve these, the Pensnett Canal was built in 1840. This short canal connected with the Dudley No 1 line at the top of Parkhead locks. Coal from the mines was brought to Wallows Basin by standard-gauge mineral railway; there loads were transhipped into the canal boats. This photograph, taken in 1927, shows the distinctive privately owned waggons (ED) unloading into typical BCN day boats. The wharf crane is a very fine example. The Pensnett Canal fell into disuse in the early 1940s, although a short section survived until 1950 before it was finally abandoned.

43 The Dudley Tunnel is the longest canal tunnel still usable in this country. Finished in 1792, it is 3154 yards long. Part of it is unlined and

hewn through solid rock. It was a very small-bore tunnel, which meant that boats could not pass in it, hence they were allowed through on a timetable. The tunnel carried a great deal of trade in its day; for example, in 1853 41,704 boats passed through — ten for every hour of the day, which is good going as they all had to be legged. In 1858 Netherton Tunnel was built some miles away but parallel, and this took a lot of the Dudley traffic. Interesting features of the tunnel were branches leading away from the main bore to serve mines or quarries. The most famous of these was the 1,227 yard side tunnel to Wrens Nest basin. Limestone mined from this point was taken out to be burnt in lime kilns alongside the canal and on the nearby Lord Ward's canal. This photograph of 1905 shows the canal to the Wrens Nest, leading out of Castle Mill basin. The chains on the wall were for boatmen to hang on to, while the boards stacked on the right are stop boards for inserting into the tunnel mouth, should it be necessary to drain the tunnel.

44 In 1950 the last commercial boat passed through the tunnel, and in 1962 the canal was officially abandoned. Thanks to the efforts of the Dudley Tunnel Preservation Society (now the Dudley Canal Trust) the tunnel has been repaired and was re-opened in 1973. Lime from the quarries in the tunnel and elsewhere came to these kilns on Lord Ward's Canal. They were built in 1842 and as can be seen boats can be brought right up to their base. It is thought that the structure on top of the kilns is a steam powered crane used for charging the kilns. The structure in the foreground is a screw elevator and grader which was used to load both boats and wagons. These kilns and part of the screw elevator structure form a major feature of the Black Country Museum, an open air museum which now occupies this site.

Black Country Lime Works.

45

45 One of the principal reasons for the building of Birmingham's canals was to carry coal from the pits to the new industry. It was also coal which caused a number of closures. Here near Leacroft Wharf on the Cannock Extension Canal the pit-heads of the Hednesford collieries can be seen, but in the foreground the maintenance gangs are rebuilding the canal walls which have been badly affected by mining subsidence from the collieries behind. The date is 1934. The simple construction of the day boat can be seen, particularly the exposed knees, very similar to those on the original boats used on the underground tunnels of the Worsley Canal system. Wooden knees were used originally but with the advent of mechanical unloading devices the coal grabs tended to inflict severe damage on the knees, so they were replaced by steel ones.

46 Mining subsidence has always been a problem on canals in Birmingham and the surrounding areas. In order to shorten the route between Dudley No 1 and 2 lines near Round Oak, a new cut three furlongs long was built in 1858 and called 'the Two Lock Line'. This short cut saved about three miles on a journey. By 1894 part of the Dudley Canal, as well as the Two Lock Line, was affected by subsidence. The subsidence was dramatic indeed, for overnight part of the canal collapsed into a mineshaft. Further subsidence took place in later years and the Two Lock Line was finally closed in March 1909. This photograph shows the Two Lock Line drained immediately after closure. The damage to the walling is very clear.

47 So worried were the BCN about the possible breaching of the canal by mining subsidence that they erected safety gates at various places. These safety gates at Northwood on the Cannock Extension Canal are seen in the process of repair in 1934. There are two pairs of gates under this bridge, mitred in each direction. Should the canal be breached the movement of the water would automatically close the gates, so preventing the canal from draining. Mining subsidence so affected the Cannock Extension Canal that commercial traffic ceased in 1961; most of it was abandoned three years later. In 1960 part of the canal sunk 21 feet, due to open cast mining nearby!

NO THROUGH ROUTE

Quite a number of canals were constructed to large towns and cities and went no further. On investigation it is surprising how many were planned to go on to somewhere else, usually linking with another canal or river to give a through route and a better chance of trade. Basingstoke always seemed a strange place for the terminus of a canal, but such a waterway could be understood if it had gone on to Southampton, as planned. Had the Grand Western stretched from Taunton to the River Exe it would have made sense, but Tiverton seems rather an insignificant place at which to end a major waterway; when one realises it was only intended to be a branch of the main line it begins to take on a new light.

Another problem with the dead-end canal was that if there was a serious blockage for any reason a great stretch of it would be cut off for long periods, having no other exit. The Cromford suffered this fate when mining subsidence affected Butterley tunnel. Other canals in this category closed for all the usual reasons; lack of water, or lack of trade or, as so often happened, being bought by a railway company who took no interest in them or closed them down immediately and built over the bed, so gaining easy access to good routes. The North Staffordshire Railway's route along the narrow Churnet Valley, which replaced the extension of the Caldon Canal from Froghall to Uttoxeter in 1846, is an example of this.

48

48 One of the most difficult canals to comprehend is the Basingstoke. It leaves the River Wey Navigation at New Haw near Weybridge, and journeys 37 miles through Surrey and Hampshire to Basingstoke. Why Basingstoke, which is only now, with London overspill, becoming a town of any real size? The canal came into being as part of the dream of linking ports such as Southampton, Portsmouth and Bristol with London. It was opened in 1794, but before this date there were plans for it to be connected with both the Andover Canal and the Itchen Navigation at Winchester, so linking London with Southampton by inland waterway. None of this came to pass, so the canal had to make do with traffic to and from Basingstoke and the places *en route*. One of the chief exports from Basingstoke town was timber. This general view of Basingstoke wharf is thought to have been taken in 1905 when the canal was still just navigable. Two boats can be seen moored along the side of E.C. White & Son's timber yard.

49 This photograph shows the yard in close-up and is thought to have been taken approximately five years later. It is interesting to note that Whites' business was established two years before the canal was actually opened.

50 By 1825 the canal was already falling into decay and for the rest of its life it had a continual struggle to remain solvent. This photograph of Broadwater, near Basing, was taken in 1905. This stretch was still officially navigable at the time, although the weed in the water would make the passage of craft difficult. The walls on the canal bank in the distance are those of Basing House. It is said that while the canal was being built around the house 800 golden guineas were discovered. These were reputedly part of Oliver Cromwell's treasure, said to have been hidden somewhere in the grounds. Broadwater was a local beauty spot, and the well-used tow path has been trodden by walkers rather than the hooves of boat horses.

51 The most celebrated voyage on the canal must have been that of A.J. Harmsworth in his narrow boat *Basingstoke* in which he tried to navigate to the town of Basingstoke during the last few months of 1913. The Canal's Act of 1778 had a clause in it which stated that 'Should the canal be disused for the space of five years, the land should be reconveyed to the previous owners. . . .' As the last recorded voyage to Basingstoke town had been in 1910, Harmsworth thought he ought to try and get through, to keep the canal open for himself and other traders. On November 16 1913 *Basingstoke* left Ash Vale loaded with a token cargo of sand. One of the first major obstacles was Greywell tunnel (1,230 yards long) which had partially collapsed in 1890 but had been repaired. In this photograph the crew are shafting the boat into the tunnel but, as can be seen, a cross plank has been positioned to allow two people to lie on their backs and leg or walk the boat through the tunnel. The substantial windlass is there to help extract the boat when hard aground.

52 Early in December the boat was struggling among the reeds (bottom photograph) near Mapledurwell, 4½ miles from its objective. It was being towed at this time by one horse and at least eight men. The following account was written by *Daily Express* reporter Ivor Heald.

Little did I think when I sailed away from Mapledurwell last evening, singing shanties and waving handkerchiefs, that in a few short hours our ship would be coming back that way again, stern foremost. Alas! The canal had another bad puncture during the night, and at dawn the look-out discovered that we were running directly on a mile of dry land. One of the narrowest escapes we have had. The captain, with admirable presence of mind, immediately orders us to reverse the horse, and we ran back about half a mile for safety. . . .'

Mr Heald's report makes the whole episode sound like something from a children's adventure story book. It is thought that the voyage ended at Basing and that the boat did not get through to Basingstoke. Even so the canal was not closed on this occasion but sold.

53 This scene was taken at Crookham around 1904, when the Basingstoke Canal had been put up for sale. It is thought that the narrow boat (Lot 124) was the canal company's work boat used for canal maintenance. Previously this boat had been a trading boat which was then bought by A.J. Harmsworth and converted into a simple house boat. From 1890 he lived on it with his wife before selling it in 1895 to the canal company who converted it back again. By the time this picture was taken it can be seen to be in very poor condition. Some would call it a 'watercress bed', the boatman's term for a leaky boat.

53

54 Pontoon Building, Aldershot.

55

The Canal with Royal Engineers Yard.

54 and 55 The government confirmed in 1854 that it was going to build a military camp at Aldershot. Previous to this, the common land in the area had been earmarked for troop training. With the building of the camp over the next five years a great deal of extra trade was brought to the Basingstoke Canal in the form of building materials, so much so that the tonnages coming on to the canal from the River Wey increased from 10,669 in 1854 to 19,720 the following year and to a staggering 27,664 tons in 1856. The coming of the camp helped save the ailing canal. The presence of some 15,000 troops brought trade in the form of army supplies, hundreds of tons of oats for the horses and sometimes even a backload of horse manure. The army also used the canal for training and manoeuvres, as these two photographs clearly show. Bridge building was one of the specialities of the Royal Engineers who were stationed there and the canal has seen many temporary structures built across it during exercises. The temporary pontoon is obviously based on barrels, while in the other photograph the two craft are proper

bridge pontoons. The pictures are thought to have been taken around 1910.

56 This photograph shows two boats at the fifty yard Little Tunnel on the top part of the Basingstoke Canal, above the longer tunnel at Greywell. The photograph was probably taken in 1904 or 1905 and is believed to show the narrow boats *Maudie* and *Ada* belonging to the Hampshire Brick and Tile Company of Nateley. The boats are moored and a gang plank has been put ashore. As there was no wharf at this point it may be that the horse had been taken down the lane which crosses the tunnel to the nearby farrier for the fitting of new shoes. It is thought that the boats were built initially for the Surrey and Hampshire Canal Company around 1880 before passing into the hands of the brickworks. A number of their boats were built at Appledore in North Devon and brought round to Bristol, lashed to the side of coastal vessels, thence via the Kennet and Avon Canal and River Thames. These boats are typical of craft trading on that canal, which frequently went onto the River Thames. Most of them

had their bows built up with wash boards; these would help stop heavily laden craft from shipping water on windy reaches of the tideway, or protect them from the wash from tugs pulling them. Incidentally, they were always breasted up when on the tideway. The boats are both fitted with a small windlass on the fore end, for an anchor when working on the Thames. Note the absence of a water can on the cabin roof. Instead one boat has a water barrel, a custom more familiar on boats in the North of England but common on the Basingstoke. The traditional roses and castles come on visiting boats only; the Harmsworth family did not like them.

57 Not much is known about boat building on the Basingstoke Canal prior to 1918. It is known that A.J. Harmsworth started repairing boats at Ash Vale around 1902, and in 1918 he built the barge *Rosaline.* Soon he was building boats at approximately yearly intervals. They were constructed to his own design, based on his experience of trading on the Basingstoke Canal, the River Wey Navigation and the River Thames. The barges were 73 feet long and 13 feet 10½ inches wide, designed to carry up to 80 tons each. The pictures show the barge *Aldershot* under construction in 1932. The use of the boatbuilder's adze can be clearly seen. Although a corrugated iron shed had been built in 1925 to enable such building work to be carried out under cover, it was not in use at this time. After launching, the barges were taken across the canal to the boat repair yard where they were fitted out. It is estimated that it took four to six men 3½ months to build a barge and the cost of the *Aldershot* in 1932 was £900. The last barge was built in 1935 though repair work continued until 1947.

58 While this may be a well-known photograph it does give a good indication of the primitive methods employed when repairs were necessary on the waterways. This picture was taken as late as 1912, yet there is no sign whatsoever of mechanisation. These were the methods and the tools used for canal construction 140 or so years before. Forks, spades and shovels are used for digging while the spoil is carried away in wheelbarrows over precariously constructed 'barrow runs' to a suitable dumping ground. Some of the more important lock gates on the canal were made in oak rather than pitch pine because oak was more durable. The Harmsworth family carried out repair works on the canal before they became the owners, this work being done in lieu of tolls. The white gates here on Goldsworth IX near Woking on the Basingstoke Canal came about after a careless workman spilt white paint over part of a new gate while under construction. He was therefore instructed to paint the whole gate white. In recent times the canal to Greywell has been jointly purchased by the Surrey and Hampshire County Councils and is being actively restored by them in conjunction with Surrey and Hampshire Canal Society.

59 Many people think that pleasure boating is a relatively new pastime on the canals. However, the day hire of boats such as punts, canoes or rowing boats has been going on for many years. In 1883, for example, there were ten boat stations on the Basingstoke Canal. The one near the army camps at Ash Vale was perhaps the best known. Long-distance pleasure trips such as that described in Temple Thurston's *Flower of Gloster* were not, of course, very common. This scene shows Frimley top lock around the turn of the century. The building is the canal company's carpentry shop and blacksmith's forge. Moored outside is a steam boat with cabin, possibly used by the canal's directors; it appears in other photographs of this area, though Frimley was no doubt its home mooring. The smaller steam launch appears to be a visitor. Could it possibly be connected with the tent on the lockside?

60 In order that coastal vessels should not have to navigate around Lands End to reach the Bristol Channel from the English Channel, an ambitious canal, known as the Grand Western Canal, was projected to run from Topsham on the River Exe in Devon to Taunton in Somerset. The first survey was made in 1792 but work did not start until 1810. The first section to be made was a level pound of 11 miles from Tiverton to Holcombe. This section was one of the three branches envisaged for the main line. It was believed that this would be an easy section to make, and that there would be considerable traffic in limestone over it from Westleigh quarries to Tiverton. This picture demonstrates that parts of the canal were very straight and had a good towing path. Here we see a maintenance gang cutting weed which would choke the canal and impede the passage of boats. The cutter consists of a series of blades on a long rope, which was worked back and forth in a sawing action by men on either bank, so cutting off the weed low down on the stem.

61 As the Channel linking project faded away, it became imperative that the canal should be connected to Taunton to allow cargo to flow to Tiverton from the Bristol Channel via the Bridgwater and Taunton Canal. A tub boat canal with lifts and inclined planes was built to Taunton. The mechanics of the lifts and planes caused some trouble but more significant still, a branch railway was built to Tiverton in 1848. Within a year the through haul tonnage from Taunton to Tiverton dropped from 10,532 to 2,456 tons. In 1856 the Great Western Railway bought the canal, closing the tub boat section eleven years later. The remaining section (the original 11 miles) carried a small amount of trade up until 1924. This amounted to a few boats; de Salis in Bradshaw says two, but this picture shows three and another photograph from the same series also shows three that were engaged in roadstone and limestone traffic. Here we see them being loaded at the quarries near Loudwell at Whipcott wharf, about 1900. The boats could load 8-10 tons each. The canal horses are standing by to haul the load towards Tiverton.

61

62 Even though latterly the Grand Western Canal only carried a few thousand tons of goods a year, the Great Western Railway had to keep it in reasonable repair. A series of leaks at Halberton caused problems in the 1890s. By the end of 1905 the receipts for 6 months trading were reputed to have been £119. By the same token expenses had not been very high either at £197. Perhaps there had been no item of major repair in the months covered by the figures. This photograph, taken on 27 April 1921 near Sellake Bridge, shows that the water has drained out through the bed of the canal, leaving behind it a gaping fissure and the threat of a bank collapse. It is surprising that repairs of this magnitude were justified at this time and that a breach such as this did not close the canal for good, as it was only three years before its final closure. This section of the canal gave continual trouble through leakage.

63 Here workmen are digging out the clay bed and replacing it with new puddle in an attempt to stop some of the water loss. Again, this photograph was taken in April 1921 and near the previous location. After closure of the canal this portion was dry for many years. In recent years when the canal was being repaired, it was this section which caused the restorers the most trouble as it still leaked.

64 The Herefordshire and Gloucestershire Canal had a short and chequered career. It was quite a latecomer, and one would have thought that its promoters would have taken heed of the troubles of some other mainly rural ventures. In 1794 the canal was opened from the River Severn opposite Gloucester to Oxenhall a few miles from Ledbury. Here the line was held up while a 2,192 yard tunnel was cut. However, a series of small coalmines were opened in this area about the same time, and these gave some traffic through to the River Severn. In 1798 the tunnel was completed and the waterway reached Ledbury. This picture is one of the few photographs remaining of the canal before its eventual closure. This is Oxenhall Lock; the date is thought to be 1880.

65

65 The effect the waterway had on Ledbury was very marked. Priestley's *Navigable Rivers and Canals* says

. . the opening of Oxenhall tunnel effected an immediate reduction in the price of coals at Ledbury of no less than ten shillings and sixpence per ton; that quantity being sold for thirteen shillings and sixpence, when, before the opening of the navigation, twenty-four shillings was the price. Nor is it with the coalmines alone that this canal opens a ready communication; limestone, iron, lead, and other productions of South Wales, as well as those of the immediate neighbourhood of Hereford, may, by means of this canal, be conveyed to London, Bristol, Liverpool, Hull, and various other parts of the kingdom, entirely by water carriage.

This traffic was not enough and in 1840 (42 years later) work was started again on the section of the canal to connect Ledbury with Hereford. Hereford basin was reached and opened in 1845. This undated engraving shows a busy scene at Hereford; timber was obviously playing an important part in the cargoes of the canal, but were

the boats really that design, or is it artist's licence?

66 The Welshpool and Llanfair Railway in mid Wales is an enigma in railway terms. Here was a railway being opened as late as 1903, purely to serve a local farming community. It was narrow-gauge, and therefore its rolling stock could not pass on to the main line at Welshpool. In Welshpool it ignored the canal, which it crosses by an iron bridge. Nor was there any attempt to use it as a feeder for traffic, presumably because by then the Montgomeryshire Canal no longer prospered. This canal runs from Welsh Frankton near Ellesmere through to Welshpool and on to Newtown. It is really an amalgam of three canals, the first section having been built by the Ellesmere Canal Company to tap the rich limestone deposits at Llanymynech. The Eastern Branch of the Montgomeryshire Canal proper was built from here on to Garthmyl, and the Western Branch from here to Newtown. The Eastern branch was completed in 1797, but the Western did not follow until 1821. One of the

main structures on the route was the Berriew aqueduct below Welshpool on the Eastern Branch. It crosses the River Rhiew by two 30 foot arches, with a smaller arch at either end. In 1889 major repairs became necessary as can be seen here. The canal has been stanked off in the foreground and has a crude pump mounted in the centre of the dam. The canal water is being allowed to drain off by an overflow weir on the right to the river below. A barrow run crosses the bed on trestles, while mechanisation is provided by a series of light railway lines. In the background are some narrowboats, probably bringing in cargoes of bricks to help with the building work.

67 A surprisingly high tonnage was carried considering the Montgomeryshire Canal's rural character, the highest recorded figure being 113,580 tons in 1840-1. Railways came late into the area — which helped — but they reached Welshpool and Newtown in 1861, and thenceforward trade steadily declined. One quoted figure shows it as low as 8,992 tons in 1923, which is about the date of this photograph. Here a loaded maintenance boat from the LMS Railway Company locks down at Welsh Frankton. An attempt was made to close the Western Branch as long ago as 1876, with the possible closure of all sections in 1886, but as it was making a profit it was allowed to continue. In the light of subsequent developments it seems strange that the costly repairs to the Berriew aqueduct in the previous picture should have taken place on a section of canal leading to one known to be financially unsound. The Western Branch was closed in 1936 when the canal burst at Dandyfield. Parts of the canal are now being restored by The Shropshire Union Canal Society.

68 An unusual aspect of the traffic on the Montgomeryshire Canal was a daily fly boat service for light goods and passengers from Rednal at the bottom of the Frankton flight of locks to Welshpool and Newtown. At Rednal the boat connected with trains to Chester, Birkenhead, Liverpool and Shrewsbury. You could, for example, leave Newtown at 7 am by fly boat and be in Liverpool by 4.5 pm. An unusual craft often seen on the canal was the Shropshire Union Canal Company's inspection craft, normally based at Ellesmere and photographed here at Pant. The boat was called *Inspector* by the Shropshire Union and was used by them until 1934. Unfortunately the date of the picture is not known. *Inspector* was purchased in 1934 by a Mr Hobson-Greenwood who said that she was 'fitted out in a grand style with a long saloon and a mahogany table with drop leaves which ran the whole length of the saloon . . . the cutlery, china and cut glass were the finest and were all marked "Shropshire Union Canal Company".'

69 The Shropshire Union Canal Carrying Company was controlled by the London and North Western Railway and unlike most railway controlled companies it tried to make its canal carrying pay. By the early 1900s they had over 400 boats trading. In 1921 the Railway Unions, completely oblivious to the requirements of canal carrying, insisted that the boatmen and their families should only work an eight-hour day as did the railmen. This was the last straw, and as the fleet was not paying its way it was disbanded and the boats broken up or sold to smaller traders. The Rochdale and Leeds and Liverpool Companies gave up their carrying fleets at the same time for the same reasons. Between the locks at Welsh Frankton was the boat-building yard of Henry Egerton who later passed it on to John Beech. This yard served the needs of the smaller traders. S. Owen & Son were typical. They owned this one boat and traded from a wharf at Pant near Llanymynech. In this picture their boat *Five Sisters* has just been repainted at the boat yard. John Beech is standing in the cabin.

70

71

70 John Beech also owned a couple of boats himself and traded along the length of the canal. He is seen here standing with his family on his own boat *Olga*.

71 Another person who spent a lot of time cruising for pleasure on the canals in the 1930s was Captain J. Carr-Ellison, who, in May 1930, piloted a 12 foot open motor launch from London to Ripon in thirteen days! In 1933 a chance meeting with another enthusiast, a Mr Anglin, at Worcester, introduced him to the idea of converting a working narrow boat for cruising. Thus in 1935 Captain Carr-Ellison commissioned Salters of Oxford to make him a floating home suitable for long distance cruising. The basis for his craft was a horsedrawn working boat into which was grafted a Coventry Victor engine which normally resided in a van used during the winter months on the owner's Northumberland estate. Another import from the estates was a mare called 'Doll' who was kept in readiness if ever they were to explore waterways known to be clogged with weed. The Carr-Ellisons travelled widely. One such trip was over the Montgomeryshire Canal and they are seen here climbing through the locks at Welsh Frankton shortly before the canal was finally breached.

72 The canals of Shropshire are extremely complicated and difficult to understand. They came into being as a result of the explosion of industry in the area now known as Telford — made up of such towns as Wellington, Oakengates, Donnington, Dawley, Madeley and the most famous of all to the industrial archaeologist, Coalbrookdale. The Shrewsbury Canal was opened in 1797 to bring coal from the Oakengates area to the town of Shrewsbury. Later in life this canal was joined at Wappenshall by the Newport branch of the Birmingham and Liverpool Junction Canal, completed in 1835. This at last gave all the products of the area ready access to the Midland canal system. The Shrewsbury and surrounding canals were built initially to take tub boats because the waterway involved a number of inclined planes. These were necessary in this case because of the hilly terrain and a lack of good water supply. This picture is thought to have been taken in 1907 and shows the actions of a typical man-and-wife team as they bring their horse-drawn boat into the lock at Newport. The horse has already started feeding from his nosebag, the man has just checked the forward motion of the boat with the fore end strap around the strapping post, while the wife has jumped off and is about to close the top gate.

Canal Lock, Newport Salop

73 Josiah Clowes was the engineer initially responsible for the Shrewsbury Canal. One of the problems to be overcome in the making of the canal was the crossing of the River Tern at Longdon, some 16 feet above the level of the surrounding meadows. Clowes built out earth embankments and constructed a masonry aqueduct. While the canal was still being built, serious flooding occurred in 1795, washing this structure away. Clowes died soon afterwards and Telford took over. Using the original stone abutments he built a cast-iron trough 62 yards long by 7 feet 6 inches wide and 4 feet 6 inches deep. The cast iron plates were made nearby in the works of William Reynolds, famous ironmasters of Ketley. Reynolds is thought to have had a hand in the design. The tow path takes the form of a narrower trough alongside. This was the first major cast-iron aqueduct in the country and pre-dated the Pontcysyllte by 9 years. Telford was appointed engineer for the Shrewsbury Canal on 28 February 1795 and produced his plans for this aqueduct soon afterwards. The use of iron for Pontcysyllte was officially approved in July 1795, so it can be seen that Longdon on Tern was a trial for the larger structure. The photograph was taken in 1963 when there was still some water in it, but later the water was drained and the bed of the canal and the aqueduct used as a farm track.

74 The Berwick Tunnel is one of the features of the Shrewsbury Canal. Priestley says 'the tunnel near Atcham is also remarkable; it is nine hundred and seventy yards in length and 10 feet wide, with a towing path 3 feet wide, constructed of wood, and supported on bearers from the wall.' This picture of the Shrewsbury end of the tunnel is thought to have been taken in the 1880s. A tub boat can be seen in the tunnel mouth. The tow path was removed in 1819. Bradshaw in 1904 adds a novel twist.

There are no fixed hours for boats to pass through this tunnel. There is a white mark in the middle of the tunnel, and should two boats meet, the one who has reached the middle of the tunnel

first has the right of way.

The author can appreciate the position of two boats meeting in the centre and neither wanting to give way. It happened to him one evening in the middle of the 1¼ mile Harecastle Tunnel. A similar story is told of Greywell tunnel on the Basingstoke Canal when two boats met in the centre:

. . . neither of the captains would give way. The owner of one barge, a miller, near Odiham, sent in a boat with provisions and beer for his men, and so starved their opponents into surrender.

75 and 76 These two photographs show the top and bottom of the Trench inclined plane, part of the Shrewsbury Canal and the last plane to work in this country; it did not close until as late as 1921. It was built and open by 1794, almost three years before the completion of the rest of the canal. Tub boats were floated onto a cradle running on lines very similar to a railway. The cradles had larger wheels at the back to compensate for the angle of the plane, and in an attempt to keep the tub boat on as even a keel as possible. They also had an extra set of wheels at the front which were mounted on the outside of the framework of the cradle. As the cradle went over the cill at the top of the plane, these wheels would engage on rails on the dockside which would stop the cradle tilting to a severe angle. The picture of the top of the plane shows an unladen tub boat which has just come over the cill into the top pound and is about to be eased off into the water. The engineer in charge of the plane at the time of the photograph (standing in the doorway) was William Jones who died in 1954 at the age of 84. He was assisted by a young brakeman (standing centre) called Frank Owen who was 88 when he died in 1963. The steam engine was required to even up the loads, as it was not always possible to have a loaded boat pull up an empty one by gravity and the power of the engine was required to pull the boats over the cill at the top. The engine was renewed in 1842 and worked through until the closure 80 years later, Frank Owen claiming that it would work all day on a steam pressure of ten pounds per square inch. He also indicated that 50-60 boats moving over the plane would be considered an average for a busy day. Traffic was mainly one-way, coal going down to the Shrewsbury Canal, but an occasional cargo such as wheat came up, for Bullocks Flour Mills at Donnington, the last traffic on the plane. The heavily laden boat moored here is thought to be loaded with materials for the maintenance work which is going on and is not the next boat to go down. The original of this photograph is undated but it was probably taken around 1900. The picture of the bottom of the plane gives some idea of the rise in relation to the surrounding countryside and also its proximity to an urban area. Again the date is uncertain but it could have been as late as 1921, when the plane was abandoned. There is no sign of a cradle on either of the two lines although all appears to be in quite good repair. The warehouse on the right would have been a transhipment points for goods which came down the plane from tub boats on to narrow boats, both of which can be seen in the basin.

77 The firm of G.F. Milnes and Co, well known as tramcar builders, opened a new factory at Hadley, near Wellington, in July, 1900. As with all such organisations, an artist's impression of the new factory was prepared before the new building was completed to enable the company to publish details of their expansion. This picture is an enlargement of just part of that impression. It shows that the factory was built close to that section of the old Shrewsbury Canal between Wappenshall and Trench, near its junction with the Newport branch. While the artist may have been accurate in his portrayal of the guillotine lock gate and the fairly typical Welsh canal type bridge, he had obviously never seen a narrow boat when he drew this picture. His version bears no relation to the size of the lock. The boats in the foreground are unloading coal into the boiler house of the factory, while the dock behind is for the import of timber, for the bodybuilding side of the business.

78 The Donnington Wood Canal was the first of the Shropshire group. Some 5 miles long and on the level, it was originally intended to give access to the Newport-Wolverhampton road. In the end it was connected by the Trench inclined plane to the Shrewsbury Canal, most of its traffic going in that direction. Very little is known about this photograph of a typical tub boat of the area. Obviously the boat is out of use and pulled up on the bank of a small stream. The caption attached to it in the original album from which it was copied says 'tub boat made Lilleshall Company Limited, Old Yard Works, which closed in 1851'. The tub boats measured 19 feet 9 inches long by 6 feet 2 inches wide. They would normally carry 5 tons of cargo on a draft of 2 feet.

79 Within Shrewsbury the terminal basin was abandoned in 1922, and in 1936 the last recorded boat berthed in the town. Three years later the canal was abandoned within the limits of the town. This photograph is of the wharf at the village of Uffington just outside Shrewsbury and was taken at about the time of the passing of the last trading boat. This photograph has a timeless quality about it, but clearly illustrates the very narrow cobbled access to the wharfside. Such access was all that was necessary for a horse and cart, though no use for to-day's articulated lorry. The wharfside crane is typical. It would have been hand operated and quite capable of lifting boxes or sacks from the holds of the boats.

80 Grantham is 20 miles due east of Nottingham. It is an important town in the midst of a mainly agricultural area. In the mid-1700s all goods coming to or from the town had to be carried overland, but in 1791 a canal from the Trent to Grantham was planned. It was completed in 1797. Priestley, writing about the canal in 1831 says

The Navigation is now complete . . . and the advantages to the town of Grantham are very great; corn, timber, coals, lime, and many other articles both of import and export, by the communication open through this canal, with those of Nottingham and Cromford, are now transferred at a comparatively easy cost, giving amongst other things, to the inhabitants of this district, the comforts of fuel at a much less expense than heretofore.

The locks on the canal were built to a width of fourteen foot which allowed both Trent craft and narrow boats to trade on it. This pair of boats is moored at a wharf just outside Grantham in 1910.

81

82

81 While coal had once been a major traffic on the waterway, by the turn of the twentieth century it was being taken by rail, so much so that total cargo carried on the canal in 1905 amounted to only 18,000 tons. 8,000 tons of this, incidentally, was manure, an unusual cargo to be found in such quantity at so late a date. By 1910, the approximate date of this picture, few trade craft disturbed the waters at Ealesfield Lane Bridge, so pleasure boating and fishing took over. The building in the centre looks to be a boat repair dock or boat house.

82 In 1833 J. Rofe and his son put forward an idea to link the Grantham Canal from its terminal basin, seen here, to the Sleaford Navigation some 16 miles away, so gaining access to Boston and the east coast trade, but finance was against it and the money could not be raised. As it was, the Grantham Canal was in trouble because of the high tolls it charged. For example, corn bound for Manchester was being taken via Newark, Selby and then by railway, which was cheaper than using water transport all the way. More surprisingly, Nottingham coal, one of the original reasons for the canal's very existence, was more expensive in Grantham than coal bought in Yorkshire, taken by sea to Gainsborough, thence by the Trent to Newark, and finally overland! Trade dwindled so much that the canal was officially abandoned in 1936. The canal warehouses seen here were demolished in October 1929. The ladies in the foreground were the Misses Cameron who ran a boat hiring business from the basin in the 1920s.

83 To gather the information for Bradshaw de Salis travelled by water over 14,000 miles in eleven years. Most of the journeys, in the southern part of England at any rate, were undertaken in his steam launch. On other occasions, such as his visits to the Cromford Canal in 1897, and here on the Grantham, he used a horsedrawn working boat. Here we see him resting on a deck chair in the hold of a working boat somewhere on the Grantham Canal. The photograph clearly shows how the upright stands are fitted within the hold with the top planks running over them. Over the top planks would be fitted the cloths covering the cargo if it was of a type which would be affected by wet weather.

84 Once a canal is abandoned it does not just disappear. Disused canals need maintenance the same as operational ones, otherwise banks will burst and floods will occur. In recent years the campaigning Inland Waterways Association have always maintained that it is cheaper to keep a canal open to navigation than to fill it in and culvert the water. This photograph was taken some time around the beginning of World War II at West Bridgford, Nottingham. It shows a lifting bridge spanning the Grantham Canal which still contained a full level of water, even though the waterway had been closed for some four years. There is now an active Grantham Canal Restoration Society.

85 Melton Mowbray is now famous for meat pies, but in the late eighteenth century it was basically a small rural community with a population of under 1,700. Despite this, it was thought desirable to give the town a waterway, and one was opened in 1797 to connect it with the Soar Navigation near Syston. The River Wreak was made navigable; in the course of its 11-mile route it rises 71 feet by means of twelve locks. Again the main cargo was to be coal. Prior to its building, the *Leicester Journal* of 29 October 1785 commented that Melton Mowbray was 'paying 18d per hundred weight for coals which a water conveyance would reduce to about 9d.' This photograph is of the basin at Melton Mowbray in Burton Street. The pub on the right hand side of the street is the Boat Inn, the only landmark associated with the basin that you will still find in Melton Mowbray. Another waterway leads out of the basin on the right side. This is the Oakham Canal, completed in 1802; it had a very short life, closing as early as 1846, after a takeover by the Midland Railway. Even in its last years traffic had not been that bad for a rural canal: 31,182 tons were carried up to Oakham. Much of this was coal, which went away overland for Stamford and the surrounding areas. 4,000 tons of agricultural produce such as grain and wool were the main exports. The craft in the photograph is one of the 70-foot-long wide boats which operated on the Upper Trent and inland as far as Leicester on the Soar Navigation.

86 With the closing of the Oakham Canal and the coming of the Midland Railway, Melton Mowbray lost some of its trade. During the 1860s the canal company tried to sell the waterway, first to the Loughborough Navigation, and, when this failed, to the Midland Railway itself. As the Midland did not see the navigation as a threat they also declined the offer. The canal closed on 1 August 1877. As it was a river navigation careful attention had to be paid to the livelihood of all mill owners along the route. A watermill is no use without an adequate supply of water. The river was weired at each mill to provide a mill pond, making a convenient spot for the building of a lock. This also accounts for the large number of locks, with an average drop of six feet each. This photograph of the lock at Ratcliffe-on-the-Wreak was taken in 1906, 29 years after the canal had closed. The lock gates have gone, but the chamber is in good order. The side paddles appear to be in working order, but the level of the water in the mill pond has been maintained by providing a dam of almost the same height as the previous lock gates.

87 The Nutbrook Canal branched from the Erewash Canal near Sandiacre in Derbyshire and proceeded to Shipley Wharf. But the upper part was quite unnavigable by 1895, although trade on the lower reaches to the large Stanton Ironworks continued until 1949; three years earlier the company had bought the remains of the canal for use as their principal supply of water. The weedy nature of the waterway can be seen in this charming Victorian photograph taken just two years after the canal reputedly closed to navigation. The spectacle of boys bathing in the nude, watched by girls, goes against many of the traditional ideas one associates with this period!

88

FROGHALL.
CHURNET VALLEY.

89

Canal and Bridge, Cheddleton

CONSALL, CHURNET VALLEY

88 Beside the top lock at Etruria in the Potteries a branch canal turns off. At this junction there used to be a notice saying 'The Caldon Canal is closed but craft up to two foot draft may navigate Etruria/Hazelhurst at their own risk.' Under it was a milepost saying 'Uttoxeter 30 miles'. As the notice said the Caldon was navigable, the author tried part of it in a British Waterways-owned hire boat in October 1970. It was hard going and required the use of a crow bar to operate some of the lock paddle gear. Two years later full restoration of the waterway commenced. The Caldon branch of the Trent and Mersey was opened in 1779 to Froghall to tap the very valuable limestone deposits in the quarries at Caldon Low. The lime kilns, still situated at Froghall, are said to be some of the best and largest remaining in Staffordshire. This picture of the wharves at Froghall was taken in 1910. Narrow boats are seen being loaded with limestone, one of the principle users being the Brunner Mond Works at Sandbach in Cheshire. Traffic to these works ceased with their closure in 1920.

89 At Cheddleton, some 11 miles from the Etruria end of the branch, is a famous water-driven flint mill. Some types of pottery called for quantities of ground flints in their making and the Cheddleton Mill, recently restored, is one of the few remaining. It lies behind the buildings on the right of the picture. The photograph shows a horse boat heavily laden with limestone passing the wharf at Cheddleton; it dates from about 1910. On the left are two unusual boats. The nearest one is an ice breaker which would have been towed along the canal by a team of horses to break up the ice at times of heavy frost. A group of men rocked the boat from side to side as they went, so smashing a wider channel in the thick ice. Behind it is a maintenance boat fitted with a fore cabin, some form of mid-boat shelter as well as a rear cabin, and a very large pump mounted amidships. A restored working narrow boat is now on show outside the flint mill at Cheddleton. It was the *Vienna*, formerly with the carrying company Fellows Morton and Clayton.

90 Above Froghall the Caldon Canal uses just over a mile of the River Churnet. A horse-drawn narrow boat loaded with limestone is seen here coming off the artificial cut into the river at Consall. The canal tow path crosses the river by the bridge on the right. Under bridge 49 in the background is a flood lock to protect the canal from taking too much water should the river be in flood.

91 Narrow boat *Shannon* by Bridge 49 at Consall Forge. The flood gates are clearly shown. The boat is fully loaded with limestone and the top planks can be seen lashed to the stands. There is no cratch at the fore end, just a stand. This was common practice on northern narrow boats. The unadorned chimney was common up to the early 1900s. The brass rings so often seen these days were a fashion of number ones and became general in the 1920s. The building under the bridge is thought to be the terminus of the Consall plateway.

92 This and the following photograph are two superb pictures of the narrow boat *Dora*, belonging to Price and Son of Brierley Hill on the Dudley Canal, and are believed to be previously unpublished. Both were taken around 1900. *Dora* is seen here between Podmore's Flint Mill and Consall Forge with a cargo of limestone. The spare tow line is hanging from the cabin side close to the steerer. The round castle picture decoration on the cabin door is unusual — these are more often square. The maintenance boat in the background would appear to be an old-fashioned spoon dredger.

93 *Dora* at Consall Forge most probably on the same trip. The picture clearly shows the decoration on the helm, the special rope work and swan's neck. The number on the side of the cabin is the gauging number, possibly from the Dudley Canal. Both this and the previous picture show limestone heaped high at the fore end, also the side cloths neatly rolled along the side of the hold, there being no need to cover the cargo. This is a Midlands boat; thus it has a cratch at the fore end.

91

94 In 1802 the Trent and Mersey Canal Company opened a branch canal from Hazelhurst to Leek, in the process of which they tapped a very valuable water supply from Rudyard Lake, which, after it had flowed down the Caldon Canal, fed the Trent and Mersey, so providing water to both sides of the Harecastle summit. Commercial traffic to Leek had waned by the 1930s. There had been some coal traffic up to 1934 from Foxley near Stoke-on-Trent and there had also been a small amount of traffic down from Leek to Milton (Stoke-on-Trent) with tar, which lasted until 1939. After this date the canal was disused and under the LMSR Act it was abandoned, and sections within the town boundaries were filled in during the period 1961-3. This photograph, taken around 1900, shows Leek Basin with an Anderton Carrying Company boat moored under the overhanging warehouse. The wharf crane shows up clearly as does the wharfinger's house behind. In the background the water tank at Leek railway station can be seen. This is now all demolished as well.

95 Twenty years after the opening of the Caldon Canal an Act was granted for its extension down the Churnet Valley to Uttoxeter, hence the milepost quoting '30 miles to Uttoxeter' already mentioned. This extension, opened in 1811, was 13½ miles long and dropped down the valley by some seventeen locks. In 1846 the North Staffordshire Railway Company bought the Trent and Mersey Canal and along with it the Caldon. The new owners immediately closed the Froghall-Uttoxeter section, and laid a railway line along it. From this it is easy to see why there are few (if any) illustrations of this section of the canal taken when it was still operating commercially. One of the purposes behind the abortive extension was to service the large copper and brass works at Oakmoor. This typical Trent and Mersey style mile post was photographed in May of 1958 in the yard of Thomas Bolton and Sons Ltd, Oakmoor.

96 The stonework of the California Lock on the Uttoxeter Canal has survived the 133 years of neglect since it was last used, and is in a remarkably good condition.

97 and **98** Richard Arkwright was born in Preston, Lancashire, in 1732. He later became apprenticed to a barber, eventually setting up his own business as a barber and wig maker. Arkwright was interested in machinery, and in conjunction with John Kay he produced a roller spinning machine for cotton. In 1771 he moved to the small Derbyshire town of Cromford where he set up a large mill, driven by water wheels. In 1788 he was one of the prime movers behind a waterway to connect Cromford with the Erewash Canal at Langley Mill. The 14½ mile Cromford Canal was completed in 1794. The greatest engineering feat undertaken during its building by William Jessop and Benjamin Outram was the 3,000 yard Butterley tunnel. This tunnel had no towing path, all boats having to be legged through by the crew. It was narrow, so that wider boats coming up from the Erewash could not pass through to Cromford. Navigation could take as long as three hours, so it really was a bottle neck — and this on a canal which in 1841-2 is reputed to have carried 320,000 tons in a year. Bradshaw's of 1904 quotes:

In the tunnels of early date . . . the method of propelling boats . . . is either 'shafting' or 'legging'. . . . Legging is performed by two men, one on each side of the boat, who lie down on the forend on their backs and push against the tunnel sides with their feet. If the tunnel is too wide to admit of their reaching the side walls with their feet from the boat's deck, boards projecting over the boat's side termed 'wings' are brought into use for them to lie on.'

Thomas Frost made this rough sketch of a boat being legged through Butterley tunnel in 1845. The photograph of the east end of Butterley tunnel shows a height gauge erected to impress on crews that the tunnel had restricted headroom inside, the result of mining subsidence. The two spectators are sitting on the stop planks, used to seal off the tunnel should it be necessary to de-water it. It is interesting to see that a version of the height gauge appears on the 1845 sketch as well.

99 One of the noted engineering features of the Cromford Canal is the 200-yard-long aqueduct known as Bull Bridge over the River Amber, a road, and later the North Midland Railway. As originally built this aqueduct proved faulty and had to be extensively modified.

According to Farey's *General View of the Agriculture and Minerals of Derbyshire,* Volume III of 1816

over the Amber river at Bull Bridge, there is another very considerable aqueduct...built of shale freestone, consisting of a large arch for the river, and a smaller one for the mill

lead south of it, and also a gothick arch for the turnpike road, which, owing to its improper shape, is bulged a good deal, and on the north of the river is another arch for a private road under the canal.

Later E. G. Barnes in his *The Rise and Fall of the Midland Railway 1844-1874* says:

near Ambergate, the railway was to pass clean through the lofty embankment carrying the Cromford Canal. To meet statutory requirements prohibiting lengthy interference with navigation along the canal, the piers for the new aqueduct were laid very deep down and then built up to support an iron trough cast to the exact shape of the canal. Having been floated into its exact position, the trough was sunk without causing the least disturbance to the navigation.

This photograph was taken in 1945, but the aqueduct was demolished for road widening in the 1960s.

100

100 The promoters of the Cromford Canal had wanted it to be a through route. After its opening they planned an extension from Cromford to Bugsworth on the Peak Forest Canal, thus giving access to the north via the Peak Forest and Ashton Canals and also a new route south for the valuable limestone from the quarries around Bugsworth. Such a canal would have gone via Bakewell, but would have involved many engineering difficulties, including numerous locks. In the end the gap was bridged by a railway; the Cromford and High Peak line was opened in 1831. It was 33 miles long and was one of the most extraordinary railways in the country in that it had nine rope-worked inclines on it with conventional traction on the sections in between. The canal was included in the LMSR Act of 1944, which sanctioned abandonment. This photograph of Cromford goods wharf was taken in 1945; behind are the engine shed and repair works of the Cromford and High Peak Railway and the first of the inclines, Sheep Pasture, 1,320 yards long, rising at a gradient of one in eight and one in nine. Such inclines occasionally had a serious accident when ropes broke. A. Rimmer in his book on the Cromford and High Peak Railway says

...on 1 March 1888 when two waggons forming a descending run broke away soon after leaving the Top and ran freely down the full length of the incline. By the time they reached the bottom, they were moving very fast and failed to negotiate the curve into the goods yard at Cromford wharf. Instead, they leapt across the Cromford Canal, clearing the two tracks of the Midland Railway, which at that point are some fifteen or twenty feet below the level of the canal, and finally came to rest in a field, completely wrecked.

101 Trade on the Cromford Canal was disrupted for four years from 1889 when mining subsidence caused the partial collapse of Butterley Tunnel. In 1900 further subsidence occurred and the owners, by then the Midland Railway Company, claimed they could not afford to repair the tunnel. However, the Erewash Company, unwilling to lose the trade coming onto their canal, managed to get a Government inquiry into the problem. This inquiry drifted on; its reply did not come until 1909 when a verdict was delivered in favour of the Midland Railway. This photograph shows a busy loading scene at Cromford wharf, the head of the navigation. The picture has been inscribed by the photographer, 'Wheatcroft and Sons' wharf, August 1906'. Wheatcroft was an important carrier on the canal, even running a passenger service from Cromford to Nottingham at one time. The singe fares were 4s first class and 2s second class. The date is interesting as these pictures must have been taken after the closure of the tunnel. Thus the boats would only have been able to trade over 8¼ miles of this by now truncated system. The narrow boat *Onward* is also one of Wheatcroft's. The warehouse in the photograph was built in 1824. The horse-drawn carts seen here are typical of short haul transport for heavy loads.

102 So much of these books deal with structures or boats, that it is a pleasure to be able to include a portrait of a person who actually worked on the canal. Unfortunately, however, very little is known about this particular man, a lock keeper on the Cromford Canal. The photograph was taken in 1897 on the occasion of de Salis' visit to the Cromford. The crudity of the lock beam should be noted. It was quite common practice to use trimmed tree trunks for this purpose. The strapping post in the foreground is a particularly hefty example.

103 From Langley Mill the Cromford Canal climbs through fourteen locks in $3^1/_3$ miles. At the top of the flight is the short Pinxton branch (just over two miles long) which runs to Pinxton colliery. The locks were built to the same dimensions as those on the Erewash Canal so that wide boats could trade to the colliery wharves. A tramway from nearby Mansfield was laid to Pinxton very early in the life of the canal. This photograph is thought to date from around 1906, and shows workmen digging out Pinxton basin and removing the reeds. Presumably it had fallen into disuse, and with the closing of the tunnel it was thought that some trade might return to this branch.

103

104 The Manchester, Bolton and Bury Canal was one of a number of northern waterways built with lock sizes differing from most of the canals around it. It was originally intended to be a narrow canal, but was actually built as a wide one in the hope of joining up with the Leeds and Liverpool by extending the line from Bolton to the top of the Wigan locks. Nothing came of this Red Moss extension. Although it was a wide canal the locks were for boats only 68 feet long. Its neighbour, the Rochdale, was a standard wide canal for full length boats while the nearby Leeds and Liverpool Company built their locks above Wigan for boats only 62 feet long. This selection of craft waiting above the Nob End flight at Prestolee are known in the north of England as bastard boats. In the south they would have been just wide boats or mules. They are built on similar lines to narrow boats but to a width of 10 or 11 feet with cabins, and with a stand instead of a cratch at the fore end. For trading on the Manchester, Bolton and Bury they would have been below 68 feet in length. As on so many other family trading craft of the north the water barrel replaces the gaily painted water can. This photograph was taken in 1930 at a time when there was not a great deal of traffic on this section of the canal. It was officially abandoned in 1941 after being left waterless by the breach at Prestolee in 1936.

CANAL, NOB END, LITTLE LEVER.

105 It is surprising how much of the traffic on the Manchester, Bolton and Bury was between points on the canal itself; at one time only one sixth was coming in from other canals. This particular cargo looks like cotton from the docks at Manchester. It is obviously a light cargo as the boat is carrying so much above the hold line, even to stacking bales two deep on top of the cabin. An especially short tiller has been fitted. The water barrel behind the chimney can still be seen. The picture is thought to have been taken around 1910 and shows a wide bastard boat climbing up three of the six staircase locks at Nob End, Prestolee. This canal ran a very successful series of passenger boats which commenced operation in october 1796. Some 60,000 or so passengers a year had been carried in this way. The journey was split at the flight of locks seen here, passengers having to get off their boat and walk down the locks to board another one at the bottom, so saving time. The service closed in 1838 with the opening of the railway from Bolton to Salford.

106 This photograph of the Manchester, Bolton and Bury Canal in 1936 shows graphically the seriousness of a breach in a canal engineered along the side of a steeply sloping valley. Because it was realised that this was a potentially weak stretch of canal, a large brick built supporting wall was constructed, and the tow path deliberately put on the valley's side to give extra strength. The breach occurred a few hundred yards from the locks seen in the previous photograph. Some of the brick reinforcement can be clearly seen in this picture along with a number of railway lines. The canal owners, the Lancashire and Yorkshire Railway, did major strengthening works during the period 1881-8. In the suspended boat on the left can be seen one of the containers which were used to carry coal. This breach was never repaired and it caused the closure of the canal as a through route.

107 At first glance it would seem strange that a canal should be built to the Westmoreland town of Kendal but proposals were made in around 1760 for a waterway to bring coal in and take away the local limestone. In 1792 John Rennie submitted plans for a 75½ mile canal from Westhoughton (between Wigan and Bolton) to Kendal. By 1796 there was traffic on a section around Preston, and the following year the line was opened through Lancaster to Tewitfield. By 1800 the Lancaster Canal had, however, failed to achieve either of its objectives. It had not reached Kendal, nor had it connected with Wigan and the waterways of the south. In 1805 the final stretch to Kendal was surveyed, but the people of that town had to wait until 18 June 1819 for the grand opening. The local council agreed to construct the actual basin in the town as well as wharves and warehouses (seen here in 1897), which were set at right angles to the line of the canal as it entered. In 1824 the canal company sold some land for Kendal gas works, thus creating a coal traffic which continued for 120 years.

108 The Lancaster Canal had a number of fine engineering structures including the Hincaster tunnel, 800 yards long, seen here. As there is no tow path boats could have been legged through it; in view of the relatively short distance, however, one suspects they were shafted through with the aid of a boat hook. There are some iron brackets on the southern entrance to the tunnel to this day, which suggests that there may have been a rope or chain hung on the side of the tunnel on which the crew could pull. While the boats were being propelled through the tunnel the horses would have been walked over the top and the horse path can be seen disappearing round the wall in the centre of the photograph. This classic scene probably dates from the late nineteenth century; by the shape in the tunnel it looks as if a trading boat is coming through to destroy the peace and quiet.

109 The Leeds and Liverpool Canal had planned a route from Blackburn to Wigan which ran almost parallel to the Lancaster Canal's truncated southern section. In 1810 the canal was complete from Leeds to Blackburn; only a short length to the west was needed to complete the full run over the Pennines. Rather than duplicate the waterways, the Leeds and Liverpool promoters came to an agreement with the Lancaster proprietors to rent their southern section from them. In return the Lancaster would build a short section from Johnson's Hillock to nearby Heapey (Wheelton) which would join up with the proposed Leeds and Liverpool from Blackburn. This short section contained the seven Johnson's Hillock locks. At the other end the Leeds and Liverpool built a connection from Wigan which included twenty-one locks. All was completed in October 1816. This photograph dates from 1895 and shows two typical Leeds and Liverpool type craft waiting at the bottom of Johnson's Hillock locks on the right. On the left is the Walton summit branch, originally connecting with the tramway to Preston. Although the tramway had ceased in the 1860s traffic on this arm continued well into the 1880s.

110 This is the eastern arm of the Lancaster Canal at Preston in 1897. The picture shows two boats typical of the type which travelled on this canal. In general they were very similar in appearance to those trading on the nearby Leeds and Liverpool Canal. Length was 72 feet and width 14 feet 6 inches. Given the right depth of water they could load 50 tons. Wooden built boats died out in the nineteenth century mainly due to the lack of adequate repair facilities — they were replaced by iron hulled boats built at Preston by W. Allsup & Sons. The hold has two beams running across it to stiffen the structure, much in the same way as narrow boats had tensioning chains to stop the sides spreading when loaded. All the boats had square sterns and a very wide deck area for the steerer who had in turn a very long tiller. The accommodation was under the covered stern area, access being obtained by steps down a companion way on the port side by the stove. This stove was normally inside the cabin and features a chimney made in two sections so that it could be easily taken down when travelling under low bridges. Usually the boat had a double bed across the stern and ventilator holes called air holes were built in either side of the stern post (as can be seen here); they were closed by slides. It was not

uncommon for other beds to be fitted in as well. Family boats were usual on this canal and this one has two window boxes of flowers on the deck. The space under the foredeck was not used for sleeping but for storage of fodder for the horse, spare lines, etc.

111 A branch of the canal was built in 1826 to the port of Glasson on the River Lune, below Lancaster. This allowed the import and export of raw materials and also made it possible for some small coasting craft to come directly onto the canals. In 1826, a sloop reached Preston from the Duddon estuary with a cargo of Cumberland slate. The following year a 60-ton sloop arrived at Kendal with salt originating from Northwich on the River Weaver. This latter journey is surprising as parts of the canal were always reputed to be shallow. Here a heavily laden boat is seen near Carnforth, about 1905; possibly because of the canal's shallowness it needs two horses to pull it. It is quite likely the boatman's son who is feeding the horses. Note the detachable towing mast placed on the tow path side of the boat. Each bridge on the Lancaster Canal had a white band painted around the arch as a safety precaution.

112 Packet boats were operated from Lancaster to Preston before 1820, for in that year the service was extended to Kendal over the newly opened top section. These boats were lightly built; covered accommodation was provided for only first class passengers. The swift or packet boats on the Lancaster Canal were limited to fifty people, taking roughly seven hours to cover 57 miles.

Trading boats were on occasions converted for the carriage of passengers. These lacked the creature comforts of the packet boat but that did not matter — such occasions were the annual outings of some local organisation. In this case it is a Zion Sunday school outing to Sedgwick near Kendal, about 1904. The boat is absolutely packed and the trip has caused so much interest that many more people have come out to watch. It would appear from the construction of the rising towpath under the bridge that this was a turn-over bridge, which allowed the tow path to change from one bank to the other in such a way that the towing horse did not have to be unhitched from its rope.

113 There were problems with finishing the south end of the Lancaster Canal as well. A section had been built from Bank Hill near Wigan to Walton, but the next 4½ miles to Preston were never completed as a waterway. Instead, the gap was crossed by a tramroad with three inclines and a bridge over the River Ribble. The railway proved much cheaper to build, due to the hilly nature of the ground to be covered. One would have thought that the transhipment of cargoes at each end would quickly make the railway uneconomic, but it lasted from 1803 until 1894. Trade on the canal gradually dwindled during the twentieth century, and in 1939 a short section of the canal in Kendal was closed. Much of the canal is still open, though it is closed between Tewitfield and Kendal. The bottom section into Preston was also closed. Here we see Preston Basin in 1897 with much railway activity, although if one looks closely a loaded boat can be seen between the two lifting bridges. The shunting of the coal wagons is being undertaken by horse traction, something which was not at all unusual on many railway sidings.

The vertical lift bridges are simple in the extreme. The presence of the securely tied rowing boat is interesting, bearing in mind that this was a busy commercial waterway.

114 This photograph is practically the same view as the previous one, but taken 63 years later (1 September 1960). This was one of a number of pictures taken by a British Railways Midland Region photographer a couple of years before the whole area was demolished, filled in and built over. It shows the squalor which can quickly set in on a waterway abandoned without adequate thought to its future. The structure projecting over the wharf allows the contents of small wagons to be tipped directly into the holds of waiting boats.

112

BITS, BRANCHES AND BASINS

Inevitably with a categorization such as has been used in this book certain stretches of waterway do not fit directly into any one section, and also there are large complexes of wharves, basins, etc, which have long been closed but are all part of the scene, and show just how vast the canal trading system must have been at one time. Bugsworth Basin (Buxworth nowadays) has always held a fascination for the author ever since a hire boat on which he was travelling broke down at the entrance on a journey to Whaley Bridge. While waiting for the mechanic the time was spent looking around at the vast number of wharves, basins and tramroads, long disused.

No excuse is given for including more pictures of Foxton; ones new to the readers, it is hoped. While most other inclined planes in the country were derelict or on their last legs it really does seem strange that hardened businessmen should construct another one as late as 1900 and as elaborate as Foxton. The fact that it only lasted 12 years was due to lack of use as much as the failure of the technology involved.

115 The Grand Junction Canal had several quite long branches, most of which seemed to suffer from water troubles for one reason or another. One of these branches was to Buckingham. As originally built, the canal was in two parts. The first of these was the Old Stratford branch, 1¼ miles long, which gave the main line access to the road traffic on busy Watling Street, now the A5. This short section was completed in September 1800, with the remaining 9½ miles to Buckingham taking only another eight months to finish. Bridge Two was often referred to as Old Stratford Tunnel, but was just a long bridge under the important Watling Street. This picture was taken during repairs in 1926. There was no tow path through this bridge, so the boat horses would have had to cross the busy road above.

116 In 1840 Edward Hayes started an agricultural engineering business in Stony Stratford and became fairly well known, particularly for experiments with new forms of machinery to help the farmer. He also started to experiment with and specialise in marine engines, and by the end of the nineteenth century was building actual boats. Among his customers were the British Admiralty, the Russian Government, the French Government, and the Egyptian Government, as well as many port and dock authorities all over the world. Included in his repertoire were six tugs for the LCC fire service and a Nile stern wheeler as well as a Dead Sea pilgrim boat. Most of the craft were tugs or launches, all were built to a beam just under the width of the Grand Junction Canal; none had a draft of more than four feet. Here we see boats under construction at the yard in 1904.

117 The firm's yard was some distance from the canal at Old Stratford, so completed hulls had to be towed along Watling Street and down Wharf Lane to the water. At first the firm used horses as the motive power, but later traction engines were employed, in this case a ploughing engine. This particular craft is a twin-screw steel-plated tug destined for the Nile. It was, incidentally, still operating there in the 1940s.

118 Once on the canal bank, the boats were set up for sideways launching, the ceremony being a highlight in village life, and watched by many people. Sometimes, it is reported, the launchings went wrong and the vessels ended up wedged across the canal. Many of the boats were fitted out afloat at Old Stratford which was satisfactory provided that the added weight did not take them over the four foot depth of the canal. They were then towed down the Grand Junction to Brentford where the fitting out was completed, with funnels, masts, etc. Some boats went via the River Thames and the Kennet and Avon Canal to gain access to Bristol. One boat bound for Liverpool sailed from Brentford to Hull and then used the Leeds and Liverpool Canal to reach Liverpool. During the early 1900s nearly fifty men were employed in this yard. They would also tackle boats of up to ninety foot in length, but in such cases the craft would be shipped abroad in pieces, and assembled with the aid of the most modern prefabricated plans suplied by the Old Stratford yard. The firm ceased trading in 1925, hit by competition from more modern diesels and the large number of ex-WD craft coming onto the market after World War I.

119 The water supply for the Buckingham branch came from the Great Ouse, a river which it followed very closely. At Mountmill, approximately 3½ miles up the branch from Old Stratford, the canal and the river are in close company and often leakages used to occur in the canal bed and bank, which were at a higher level than the river. During the winter of 1919 the canal was closed and a 200-yard stretch given concrete walls and bed. Figures show that there were only some thirty boats a year trading over the majority of the length of the canal, say 750 tons in all, plus a little local traffic. One is surprised that these repairs were undertaken on what must have been a most uneconomical waterway. Even in 1919 it was still a case of hard work, with wheelbarrows and barrow-runs.

117

118

120 A good supply of water is essential for any canal. As artificial waterways can climb up and around obstacles by way of locks, it is necessary to locate one's primary source of water at summit level. One of the sources for the Grand Union Canal at Tring was water coming down from the Wendover Branch. Ever since it was built in 1797 this branch canal leaked, so much so that in 1897, a particularly dry year, the branch lost more water than it provided and was taking water from the summit of the Grand Junction Canal itself. This state of affairs was temporarily halted by the provision of stop planks at Little Tring, to be followed by the permanent stop lock featured here. There was little traffic over the branch by this time so the provision of only one paddle (because of only slight differences in levels) would not have hindered many boat crews. In 1901, however, a few boats did pass through to reach Buckland wharf some two miles further on from Little Tring. This photograph was taken about 1906.

The Grand Junction Canal Pumping Station, Little Tring
Photo Copyright, C. A. Howlett.

121

122

THE CANAL. WENDOVER.

121 This pair of boats belonged to Alfred Payne of Wendover and are seen here moored on the towpath side of the Wendover Branch at Buckland opposite the Gas Works. Buckland Wharf was situated through the bridge and to the left. The date of this photograph is not known. It could have been the brief period in 1901 when some boats were known to have travelled to Buckland or it could have been shortly before the stop lock was built in the late 1890s. The Paynes were an old-fashioned family of canal carriers. The cargo is not known but clearly needs side cloths to cover it.

122 The Wendover branch was planned purely as a water feeder, and to this end various mills in the Wendover area were bought by the canal company so that there could be no dispute over water rights. It was soon realised that it would not be too costly to make the feeder into a navigable channel, and an Act of Parliament to this effect was made in 1794. The canal ended some distance from Wendover itself, and a road was built out from the town to it. The wharf at Wendover was looking very derelict by the time this picture was taken in about 1910.

123 Once the dry weather was over, such water that continued to flow down the branch was directed into Wilstone reservoir, to be pumped back up to the main line. The flow along the Wendover feeder was between fourteen and forty-two locks a day. Although a trifling amount, the Grand Junction Canal Company went to great lengths and expense to keep it flowing. In 1904 the top four miles of the canal were repuddled with clay, the water level lowered and the whole used purely as a water channel taking the water direct to Wilstone reservoir. Unfortunately, this now put an extra strain onto the pumps at Tringford, which had to lift the water as much as seventy-five feet. Instead it was decided to lay a pipeline down the disused section of the canal from Drayton to the pumping station, so taking the precious water direct to the pumps.

124 This was soon found to be unsatisfactory due to the rate of variation in the flow, which played havoc with the pumps. The whole system was redesigned in 1912, the water being pumped direct into the main line, or allowed to flow into the Tringford reservoir, which was at a higher level than the one at Wilstone. This photograph, taken on May 30 1912, is believed to be the first day the new system came into operation, and it shows the intake from the water channel at Drayton.

125

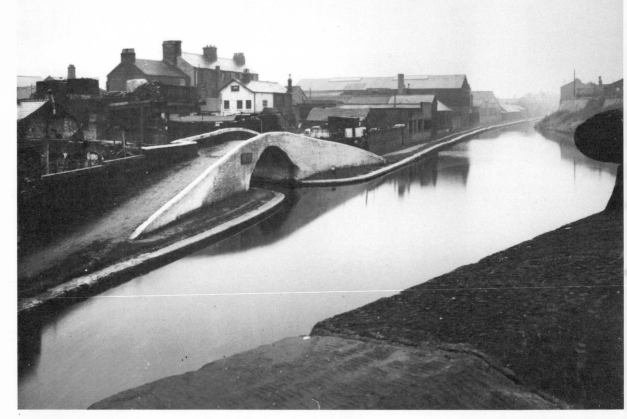

126

Stafford from the River.

125 The Newcastle-under-Lyme branch of the Trent and Mersey Canal used to leave the main line in Stoke-on-Trent. It was exactly four miles long. Most of the trade on it, according to Bradshaw, was over the first mile or so to other wharves in Stoke. It was leased to the North Staffordshire Railway, owners of the Trent and Mersey, in 1863. Nowadays, with clean air acts and active water authorities, we tend to forget that at one time parts of the canal system in this country were very badly polluted. The following account of the canal at Newcastle-under-Lyme was taken from an inquest recorded in the *Staffordshire Times* of 15 May 1875:

The water in it was inky black, and the stench intolerable. Large bubbles of gas were continually rising to the surface, being unmistakable proof of decomposing animal and vegetable matter. Three or four drains were running into it, and he saw the carcases of several dogs in various stages of decomposition floating about.

This scene of the junction of the Newcastle-under-Lyme Canal and the Trent and Mersey was taken in 1960.

126 The Staffordshire and Worcestershire Canal does not actually enter the town of Stafford. The canal was opened throughout, from the Trent and Mersey Canal at Great Haywood to Stourport on the River Severn, in 1772. As late as 1816 the canal company leased land and river access from Lord Stafford, to build a one mile navigation into Stafford itself. It left the main line near bridge 101 (Weeping Cross) and then went through Baswich (St Thomas) lock which lowered the canal to the River Sow. From here on the river was made navigable. Traffic coming in was mainly coal, and a special coal wharf was built as well as one for timber. In this picture, taken from a postcard of 1905, the River Sow is to the right, the building on the left is the Royal Brine Baths (recently demolished), and there is also a small wharf on the riverside. The tow path is in the centre of the photograph with the canal on the left. The very edge of the coal wharf can be seen. Traffic ceased on this branch some time during the 1920s although it does not seem to be very busy at the time of this picture.

127 A canal to Bradford was mooted before the Leeds and Liverpool Canal, to which it was eventually joined. In 1744 a group of 'Gentlemen, farmers and other inhabitants . . ., tried to obtain powers to make the River Aire navigable because of '. . . the heavy charges of land carriage, occasioned by the badness and unevenness of the road. . . .' The Bradford Canal, as finally built, was 3⅜ miles long, included ten locks, and was opened in 1774. The original terminus was on the edge of the town, but with added prosperity the town soon extended and the basin became much more central. As with so many canals, coal was a principal cargo, as was limestone from the Springs branch of the Leeds and Liverpool Canal at Skipton. Stone also featured as one of the principal cargoes. The closure of the canal was caused by unusual circumstances. The feeders for the canal head gradually became polluted as the urban area expanded '. . . the noxious compound is conveyed through the sluices into the canal'. An outbreak of cholera in 1849 caused the public to complain about the canal, but it was not until 1867 that it was closed and then drained. This painting by N. S. Crichton depicts the canal basin prior to its closure. It gives a good impression of the cramped nature of the then terminus.

128 The Bradford Canal was closed when it was carrying over 125,000 tons a year. Somehow the local business interest had to find alternative transport. A new company was formed and took over the drained canal, selling off the top ⅜ths of a mile, and making a new terminus lower down. Water was supplied from independent reservoirs or by pumping, so doing away with much of the pollution problem from above. The canal re-opened in 1873, but the damage to trade had been done. Many of the traders had found alternative ways of moving their products, and it was not until 1910 that the tonnage carried ever exceeded 100,000 tons in a year. The canal closed on 25th June 1922. Here in about 1900 *Victoria* of Bolton Woods (between Shipley and Bradford), owned by Butcher and Waterhouse, loads stone setts at Stonebridge. *Victoria* is a typical square sterned Leeds and Liverpool short boat built in Yorkshire with Yorkshire style square wooden chimneys in two sections, fore and aft.

129 In 1894 the Grand Junction Canal Company bought the Grand Union Canal, which extended from Norton Junction near Braunston through to Foxton and the Old Union Canal from Market Harborough to Leicester. This stretch of canal was generally in poor condition, but it was bought primarily as a water supply for the Grand Junction. The directors of the Grand Junction were persuaded by Fellows Morton and Clayton that traffic from the Nottinghamshire and Derbyshire coalfields to London could again be attracted to the canals, if this line were improved to take wide boats throughout. Rather than widen the water-consuming flight of locks at Foxton a plane was built instead. Gordon Thomas, the Grand Junction's engineer, was responsible for devising this plane and selling the idea to the canal company. The narrow boats were floated into two caissons full of water, one at the top and the other at the bottom, which were then pulled up or lowered down the plane. Gordon Thomas and his wife (centre) are seen inspecting the plane as it is under construction.

130 At the bottom of the plane two docks were built, into which the caisson descended. A guillotine gate was opened at the end of the caisson and the boats were then floated out. This photograph and the one which follows were both taken on the same day, possibly opening day, July 10 1900. The specially adapted maintenance boat belongs to the Grand Junction Canal Company, and there are crowds of people watching from the bridge in the distance. In this picture the caisson is just dropping into the bottom dock. A loaded narrow boat awaits its turn to ascend when the directors have finished their inspection. There are two boat horses and boatmen on the tow path, and the horse by the bridge appears to be wearing the traditional crotcheted ear protectors. Under the brick bridge can be seen the smaller swivel bridge erected to give tow path access to the bottom of the plane, and which still exists.

131 Earlier in the day the inspection party had taken a trip up the plane. They are seen here having just come out of the caisson into the canal proper. At the summit the caisson was pulled up in line with the top level of the canal, and a hydraulic ram then pushed it the few inches sideways to give a near watertight join. Hydraulic power was also used to raise the guillotine gates on both the docks and the caisson. It is claimed that the complete operation of the plane took twelve minutes, which would have saved nearly an hour over the use of the Foxton locks. The locks were a staircase, a flight of five, a passing pound and another set of five, and it was this lock configuration and not the number of locks which caused the hold-ups in busy periods.

132 What excitement for an outing actually to go up and down the inclined plane! This undated picture shows a pair of Northampton-based horse-drawn boats loaded with trippers on their way to the summit, the caisson having just left the wet dock at the bottom. It is surprising how leak-free the watertight guillotine gate is. Foxton inclined plane had been built in the hope that traffic over it would exceed 200,000 tons a year, but this never happened. Between 1905 and 1910 it varied between 31,417 tons and 40,767 tons. By 1908 it had been found that it was not economic to keep the engine in steam 24 hours a day, so night working was abandoned and because of this the locks were put back into good order. Gordon Thomas in his paper on the plane wrote

the capacity of the lift, allowing twelve minutes for each operation, and passing 70 tons in both directions, is 8,400 tons per twelve hours, or, approximately, 250,000 tons per annum of 300 working days. The cost of dealing with this tonnage, based on the experience of the last six weeks, inclusive of coal, oil, stores and labour, would be .05d or 1/20 of a penny per ton. The whole of the plant is operated by three men.

133

134

133 and **134** Bugsworth (later Buxworth) basin, near the head of the Peak Forest Canal at Whaley Bridge, must have been one of the largest wharf complexes on the British Canal system. On 1 May 1800 the Peak Forest Canal was opened, though a tramroad connected the top and bottom of what are now the Marple flight of locks. The quarries around Bugsworth were rich in limestone. One of the first people to use the basin was Samuel Oldnow who had lime kilns at Marple. Oldnow was one of the main promoters of the Peak Forest Canal because of his lime interests. These two commercial postcards, believed to date from around 1914, show Bugsworth when the tramways were fully occupied bringing limestone from the quarries. A guide book published in the late nineteenth century described Bugsworth as '...a thriving inland port. The basin...holds upwards of twenty longboats, it has a loading shed and stables for upward of forty barge horses.' The latter remark is interesting as it seems to imply that more than twenty boats could be accommodated. Although there is

only one boat visible here, some idea of the amount of traffic that this basin could carry can be gained from the lines of loaded waggons and piles of limestone. At its zenith Bugsworth village had a population of nearly 300 people; nearly all of whose employment was in some way connected with quarries, limestone or the canal.

135 This photograph shows part of the complex of wharves and warehouses at Bugsworth around 1930 after trade from the quarries had ceased and the scrap men had removed the hundreds of tramroad waggons which had littered the sidings. The building on the right is a warehouse into which ran another arm of the canal. The tramway lines are clearly seen behind, leading up the valley. By the far building on the right (a tramway workshop) a branch turned sharp right to tunnel through to Barren Clough Quarry. The main line of the tramway continued up the valley to Dove Hole Quarries 6½ miles away. In the centre of the picture are lines of the tramway which can be seen ending in a raised section by the wharf. The structure

at the end of this is a waggon tippler for unloading direct into waiting boats. On the left can be seen the bottom of the lime kilns which were normally discharged straight into the boats. Behind centre the bread van is delivering to one of the two pubs on the site. The wharves have been derelict since this picture was taken, though the basin is now being painstakingly, if slowly, restored by the Inland Waterways Protection Society.

136 The tramways leading to Bugsworth Basin were interesting. They were of the usual Outram plateway type to a gauge of 4 feet 2 inches. Working in this area of the Peak District must have been arduous. The plateway was some 6½ miles long and included an 85 yard tunnel, and a 209 feet inclined plane. The tramroad rose to a height of 1,139 feet. The canal company controlled the plateway as well as the quarries, and from all accounts seems to have been a good employer, even down to providing a store which sold their workers goods at cost price. This photograph was taken around 1905 and shows a typical horsedrawn tramroad truck on the Peak Forest system, although in this case a human cargo takes the place of limestone.

137 On 21 March 1776 the Bridgewater Canal was opened through to the hamlet of Runcorn, the point which the Duke of Bridgewater had chosen as his terminus and where he built a flight of locks taking his canal down to the River Mersey. The coming of the canal to Runcorn had the effect of

doubling the population in the years between 1801 and 1821. The traffic on the Runcorn flight of locks was so great that a second set of locks was built in 1827. With the coming of the Manchester Ship Canal, the Bridgewater Navigation Company, owners of the Mersey and Irwell, sold out to the Ship Canal Company. The route of the Mersey and Irwell was required for the ship canal. With the completion of the Ship Canal in 1894 the locks were cut off from the River Mersey, but this made little difference to the traffic. Over more recent years the pattern of trade changed and in 1939 the original locks (the old road) were closed. By 1963, the date of this photograph, the new road was practically derelict. In this picture, taken from Waterloo Bridge, the remains of the old road can be seen on the right. The River Mersey is in the background and the Manchester Ship Canal can just be seen at the bottom of the flight of locks.

138 Narrow boats used to congregate in the dock at the foot of the flight of locks. It was a favourite place to find boats from the

Anderton Company, as we see here. This scene is typical, with two families talking while awaiting another cargo. This firm started as Alexander Reid and Company and changed to Anderton Company in 1836, a name which it retained even after merging with the Mersey, Weaver and Ship Canal Carrying Company as late as 1954. The fleet was sold to British Waterways in 1958. The reason for the success of this company at a time when so many other carrying concerns went to the wall was that they kept to a regular series of routes, using customers who mostly had canalside factories and works. The Anderton Company specialised in cargoes for the potteries, bringing up from the docks many different bulky cargoes such as china clay and stone. The cargoes down to the docks from the Five Towns would normally be crates of earthenware and crockery. The boat's name, carved into the counter, was a feature of the Anderton boats as were their rounded sides, rounded because when loaded with light top-heavy crates, they would roll easily, but always come upright.

139 We are lucky to have a record of what is possibly the last ever journey up the flight of locks at Runcorn, which was accomplished by John Seymour in a British Waterways pleasure boat some two years after the Bridgewater Company thought that they were impassable! Here is an extract from his excellent book *Voyage into England*.

The locks looked not only dry, but wrecked. They were rubbish filled, and many of the gates were perished and broken. The short pounds between them had been partially filled in with sunken Bridgewater barges and these, mudfilled, had started to fall to pieces... and the whole scene was desolate and sad, yet the locks had been perfect when I had gone up the flight in *Jenny the Third* only seven years earlier...at that time there had been a fleet of narrow boats, loaded with coal, waiting there [at the top] and we had made friends with an old lady and a young girl who worked on one of them. Now there were no working boats...

The locks were in good working order when De Salis climbed them in *Dragon Fly*, seen here in June 1895.

40 Before readers pick up their pens and write to the publisher, the author readily acknowledges that he is stretching his rules by including this picture. The *Warrington Guardian* for Saturday 11 July 1874 had an item as follows:

The Bridgewater Canal Navigation Company have this week inaugurated what will no doubt prove to be a useful and profitable improvement. They have placed on the canal a screw tug steamer to be followed speedily by others for the purpose of dragging their barges, thus superseding horse power.

Eventually some twenty-six of these very distinctive canal tugs were in service. Their home was the area round the top lock at Runcorn and Waterloo Bridge. In fact they used a dry dock under the arch of the bridge on which the photographer is standing, and it is this dry dock and the section of the canal beyond which no longer exists today. This photograph shows at least thirteen of these tugs preparing for a day's work in around 1910. The tugs never worked down the Runcorn flight with a tow, as no craft were allowed down under power (they had to be bow-hauled). They did tow boats on the Manchester Ship Canal, also on the Mersey and Irwell Navigation. It can be seen that the tugs have wheel steering at the stern. Access to the smoke box (for sweeping the tubes) is through the hatch in front of the funnel (open on left hand boat).

141 Apsley South End Wharf at the Dickinson paper mill in Hertfordshire must have been typical of so many factory wharves up and down the country in the days of commercial traffic. John Dickinson's fleet of boats was owned by Fellows Morton and Clayton and worked a regular run from Apsley, Nash, Home Park and Croxley Mills down the Grand Union to Dickinson's Paddington depot. Their principal cargoes were finished paper products down to Paddington, and rags and similar waste products up to the mills for pulping. The boatmen on this run were often known as 'the paper dashers'. The circular chimneys suspended from the roof are a relic from the days when steam-powered narrow boats operated from the wharf. The steamers used to lie with their funnels immediately under one of these chimneys. With the cessation of commercial traffic to this wharf in the 1950s it fell into disuse.

INDEX